THE ENCYCLOPEDIA
WINDOW FASHIONS

1000 decorating ideas for Windows, Bedding and Accessories.

CHARLES T. RANDALL

ILLUSTRATED BY
Patricia M. Howard

COVER DESIGN BY
Abbott Art
Santa Ana, California

Published by

 **RANDALL**
I N T E R N A T I O N A L

Randall International
P.O. Box 1656
Orange, CA 92856 USA

The Publisher has made every effort to ensure that all instructions given in this book are accurate and safe but cannot accept liability for any resulting injury, damage or loss to either person or property whether direct or consequential and howsoever arising. The Publisher will be grateful for any information which will assist us in keeping future editions up to date.

ISBN 0-9624736-8-5   Plastic spiral bound with index tabs.
ISBN 0-9624736-9-3   Perfect bound/paperback edition.

Printed in Singapore

How to reach us:
Phone: (714) 771-8488
Toll Free: (800) 882-8907
E-Mail: sales@randallintl.com
Internet: http://www.randallintl.com

CONTENTS

INTRODUCTION

"The eyes are the windows of the soul" is an often quoted poetic expression. The windows in a house, however, can often be an expression of less than perfection—poetic or otherwise. To help you achieve your own perfect window treatment is the goal of the *Encyclopedia of Window Fashions.*

Is one picture worth a thousand words? Graphics have always stimulated the creation and communication of ideas. The uniqueness—and success—of the *Encyclopedia of Window Fashions* lies in combining the presentation of 1000 illustrations with a truly encyclopedic knowledge of window treatments. Ten years and half a million copies later, this original publication remains the best organized, most effective design aid available. If your profession is interior design, this new, expanded edition belongs in your library, on your work table and with you in the field.

Visual definitions of a particular window treatment are immediately effective communication tools. When accompanied by specific yardage requirements, by glossary-supplied performance summaries of fabric properties and appearance and by alternative approaches to creating a desired effect, you have all the information necessary to work with your client. Whether a budget is lavish or modest, the *Encyclopedia of Window Fashions* offers the optimum number of choices in an individual design situation.

If this is your introduction to *Encyclopedia of Window Fashions*, welcome! Our book is sure to become an indispensable resource tool in your work. If you are among the many who own an earlier edition, I extend my sincere appreciation. Without your patronage, our latest version would not be possible. I know you will find that it continues in the high tradition you have come to expect from us.

Charles Randall
Publisher and Author

WINDOWS WITH A CHALLENGE

007A

Door with Window & Sidelights

007B

SOLUTION 1

007C

SOLUTION 2

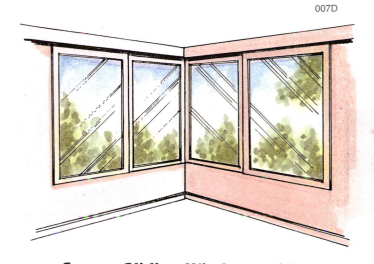

007D

Corner Gliding Windows with Structural Beam on Top

007E

SOLUTION 1

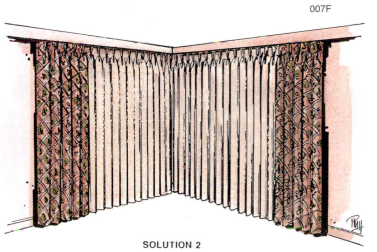

007F

SOLUTION 2

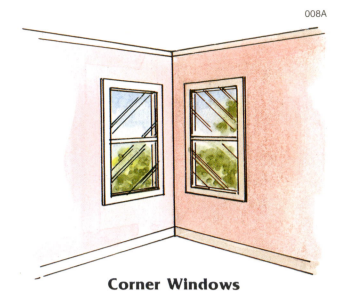

Corner Windows

SOLUTION 1

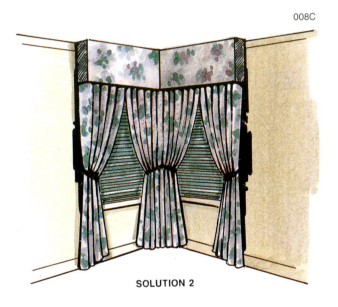

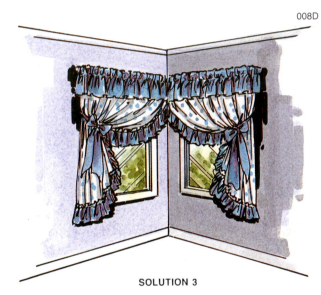

SOLUTION 2

SOLUTION 3

SOLUTION 4

SOLUTION 5

009A

Air Conditioner in a Double-Hung Window

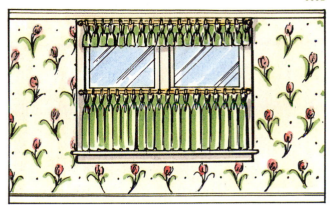

009B

SOLUTION 1

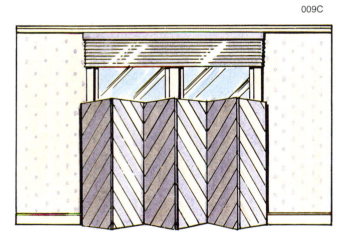

009C

SOLUTION 2

009D

Sliding Glass Doors & Cathedral Windows

009E

SOLUTION 1

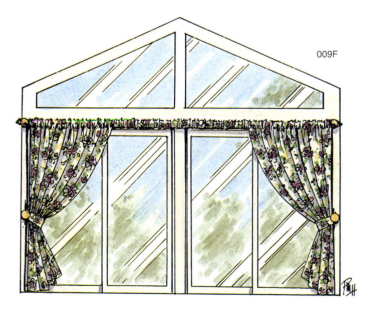

009F

SOLUTION 2

Cathedral Windows

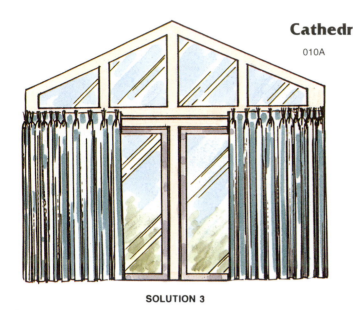

010A

SOLUTION 3

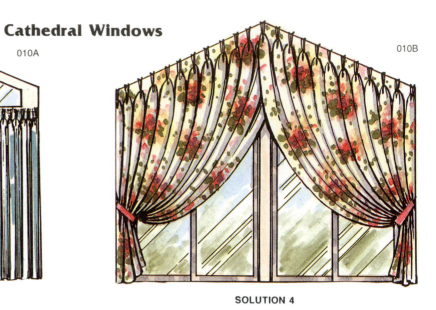

010B

SOLUTION 4

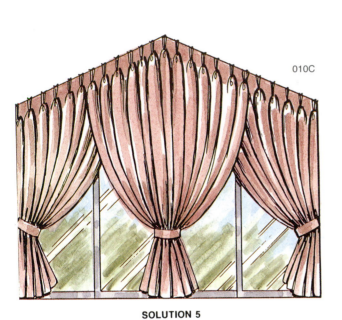

010C

SOLUTION 5

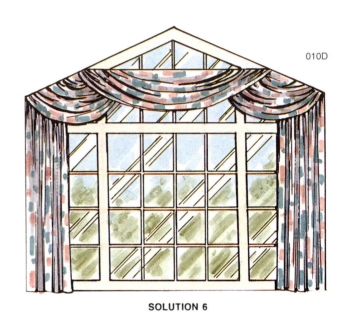

010D

SOLUTION 6

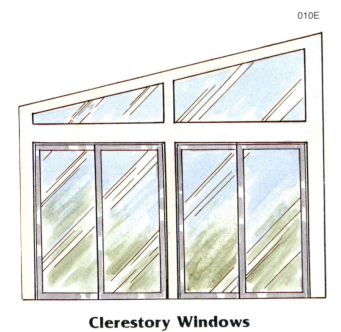

010E

Clerestory Windows

010F

SOLUTION 1

Bay with Casement Windows

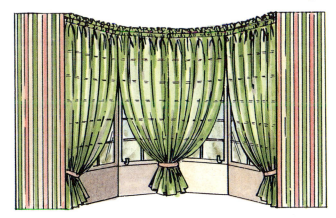

011B

SOLUTION 1

011C

SOLUTION 2

011D

SOLUTION 3

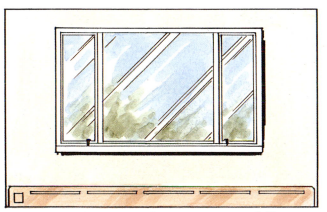

011E

Picture Window with Baseboard Heater

011F

SOLUTION 1

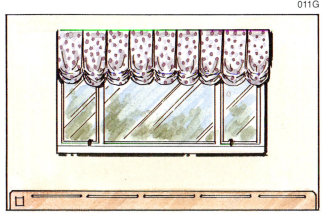

011G

SOLUTION 2

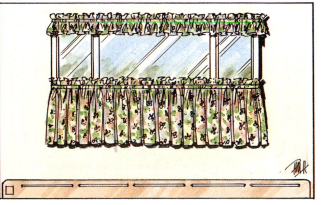

011H

SOLUTION 3

11

012A

Jalousie Windows & Doors

012B

SOLUTION 1

012C

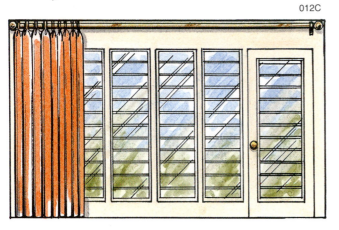

SOLUTION 2

012D

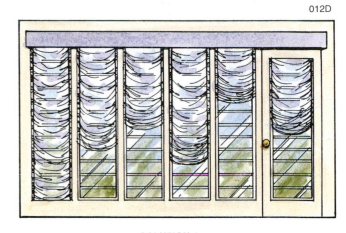

SOLUTION 3

012E

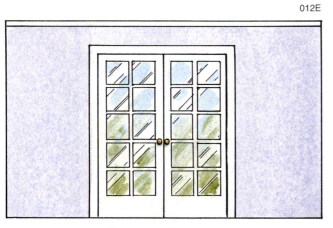

French Doors

012F

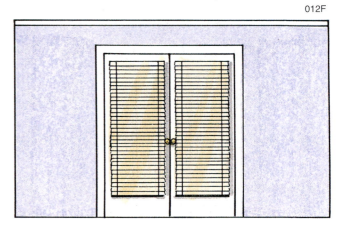

SOLUTION 1

012G

SOLUTION 2

012H

SOLUTION 3

Triple Double-Hung Windows

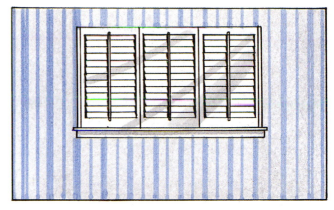

SOLUTION 1

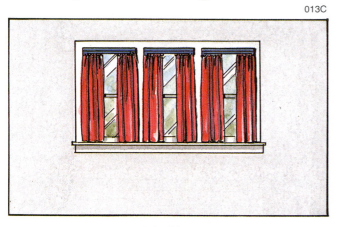

SOLUTION 2

SOLUTION 3

Bay with Double-Hung Windows

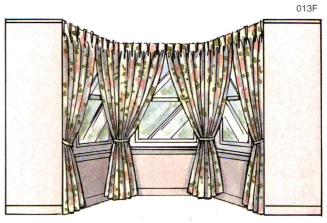

SOLUTION 1

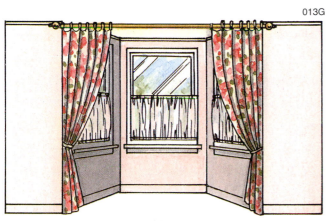

SOLUTION 2

SOLUTION 3

014A

Arched Top Windows

014B

SOLUTION 1

014C

SOLUTION 2

014D

SOLUTION 3

014E

SOLUTION 4

014F

SOLUTION 5

DRAPERIES

015A

Rod Pocket Draperies under Knotted Scarf Swag

015B

Gathered Draperies over Swag

015C

Arched Pleated Draperies

015D

Arched Swags over Arched Pleated Draperies

016A

Arched Bishop Sleeve

016B

Arched Rod Pocket Drapery

016C

Arched Knotted Swag Drapery

016D

Arched Drapery

Gathered Drapery over Austrian Shade

Tab Draperies under Swag

Arched Draperies with Ruffles & Large Ties

Rod Pocket Draperies with Banding

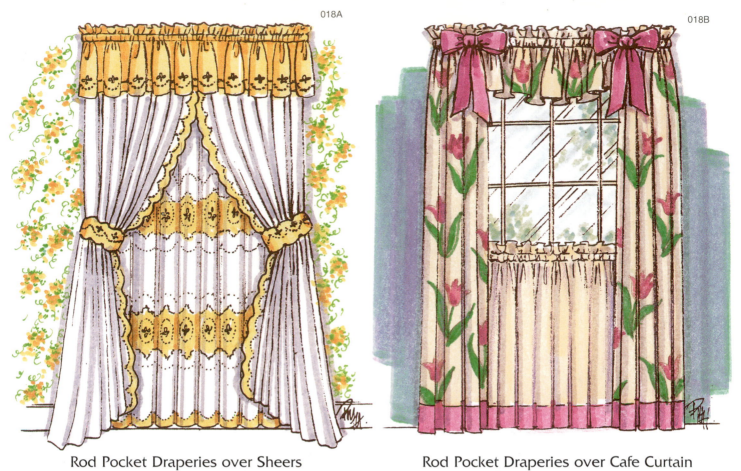

018A

018B

Rod Pocket Draperies over Sheers

Rod Pocket Draperies over Cafe Curtain

018C

018D

Rod Pocket Bishop Sleeve Draperies

Arched Rod Pocket Draperies over Cafe Curtain

Pleated Drapery on Dec. Rod with Tassels & Rope

Rod Pocket Drapery over Sheer with Tab Valance

Double Rod Pocket Drapery Tied Back

Tab Draperies on Dec. Rod

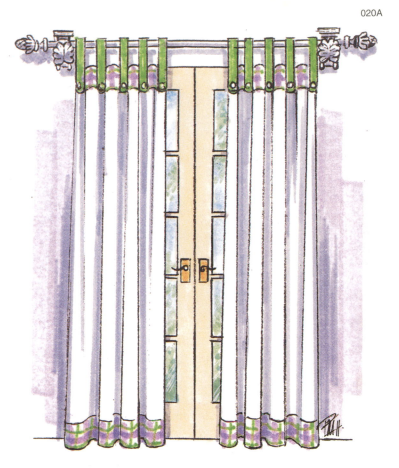

Tab Draperies on Dec. Rod with Sconces

Tab Draperies on Dec. Rod with Holdback

Tab Draperies on Dec. Rod with Holdbacks

Double Tab Draperies on Dec. Rod with Holdbacks

021A

Arched Bishop Sleeve Draperies over Balloon Shade

021B

Knotted Lace Swag over Lace Draperies

021C

Arched Gathered Valance over Draperies

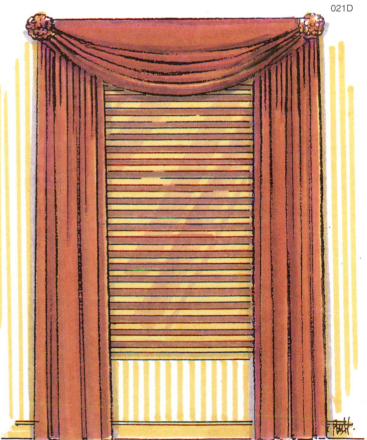

021D

Single Swag with Rosettes over Draperies

Tabbed Draperies with Valance
on Dec Rod

Gathered Draperies with Sleeve
on Dec Rod

Draperies on Dec Rod with
Special Swag Effect

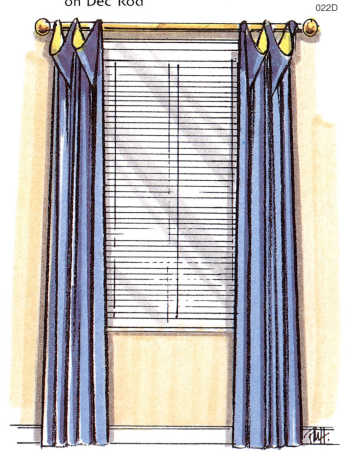

Draperies on Dec Rod

023A

Gathered Valance over Bishop
Sleeve Draperies with Cafe Curtain

023B

Single Swag over Draperies
and Cafe Curtain

023C

Sheer Valance over Tie Backs

023D

Gathered Valance over Draperies

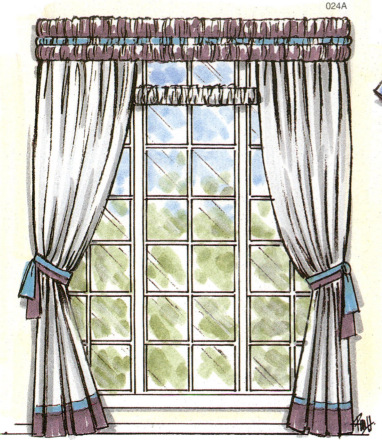

024A

Gathered Valance over Tie-backs

024B

Gathered and Swagged Valance over Tie-backs

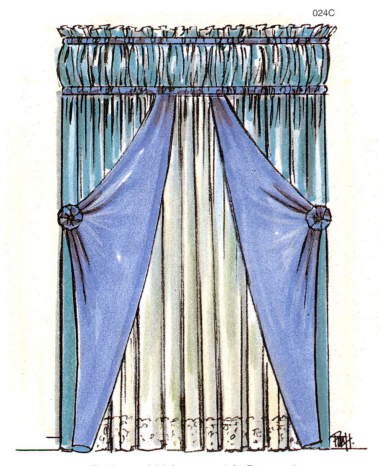

024C

Gathered Valance with Draperies Pulled Back

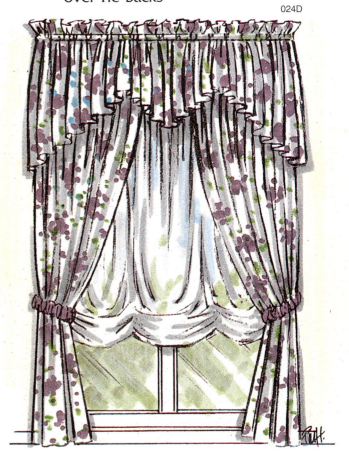

024D

Double Arched Valance over Tie-backs & Cloud Shade

Pleated Arched Valance over
Tie-backs and Sheer Balloon

Gathered Top Arched Valance
over Bow Tie-backs

Double Gathered Valance with
Brass Rod in Middle over Blind

Tabbed Drapery with Bows
& Tie-back Holder

Tabbed Drapery Tied Back on one Side

Pleated Draperies Tied Back

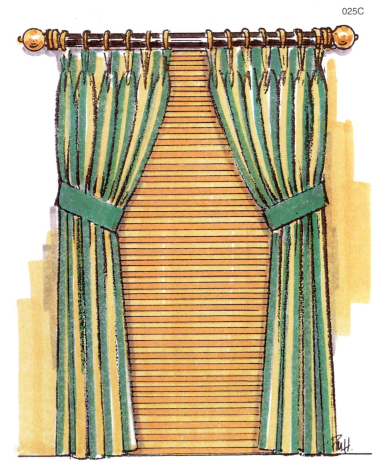

Pleated Tie-back Draperies on Dec. Rod

Rod Pocket Drapery with Tie-backs

027A

027B

027C

Alternate Heading Styles

Rod Pocket Drapery with Center Sleeve & Tie-Backs

027D

Double Rod Pocket Drapery

027E

Bishop Sleeve Draperies with Valance

028A

Arched Valance with Ruffle & Ruffled Tie-backs over Cafe Curtains

028B

Tie-back Draperies with Balloon Valance

028C

Rod Pocket Drapery with Banding

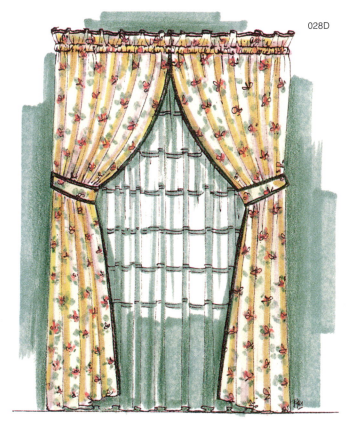

028D

Tie-backs with Ruffle at top, Sheers under

029A

Flat Rod Pocket Drapery Tied Back

029B

Rod Pocket Drapery over R.T.B. Cafe

029C

Rod Pocket Tie-backs with Ruffles

029D

Rod Pocket Valance with Rod Pocket Cafe

Rod Top & Bottom Valance with Matching
Tie-bands and Mini Blind

Flat Rod Pocket Drapery over
Rod Pocket Cafe

Flat Rod Pocket Panels with Standup Top

031A

Kingston Valance over Tied-back
Draperies & Sheers

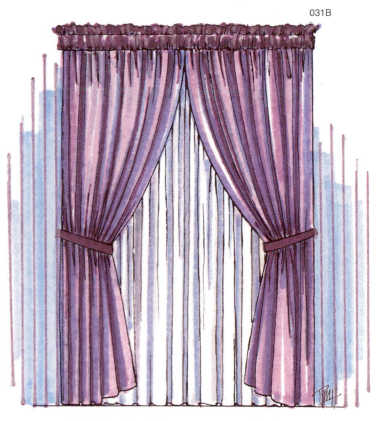

031B

Rod Pocket Drapery over Sheers

031C

Banded Stationary Bishop's Sleeve
over Mini Blind

031D

Stationary Drapery on Covered Rod
with 3" Stand-up Top

Tied-back Stationary Draperies on Dec. Pole
with Sleeve in Middle

Rod Top Draperies on Dec. Pole

Bow-tied Bishop Sleeve Draperies
Gathered on Dec. Rod

Stationary Rod Top Draperies on Dec. Pole,
Sleeve in Middle

Cluster Pleated Valance on Dec. Rod with
Pleated Draperies over Roman Shade

French Pleated Draperies on Dec. Rod
over Balloon Shade

Tab Draperies on Dec. Rod over
Cafe Curtain

Arched French Pleated Valance
& Tie-backs

Multiple Arched Valance over
Draperies & Sheers

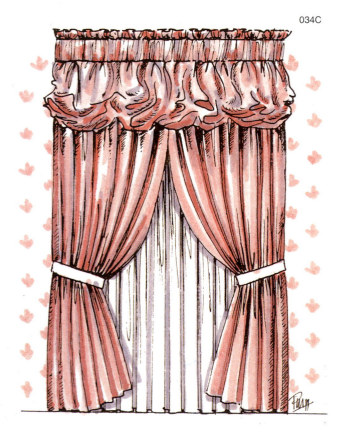

Rod Pocket Cloud Valance
Tie-back Draperies over Sheers

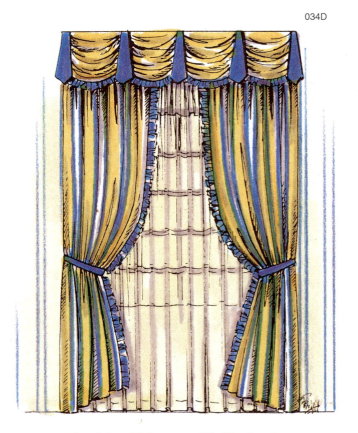

Austrian Valance with Tie-backs
over Sheers

035A

035B

Rod Top Draperies with Center Florence
& low Tie-backs over Mini Blind

Draperies Gathered on Dec. Pole
over Austrian Shade

035C

Rod Top Draperies with Multiple Bow Ties over Roman Shade

Pleated Tie-back Draperies

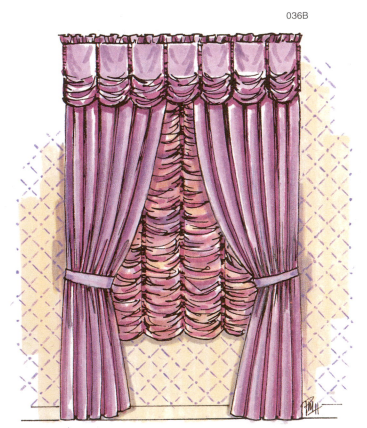

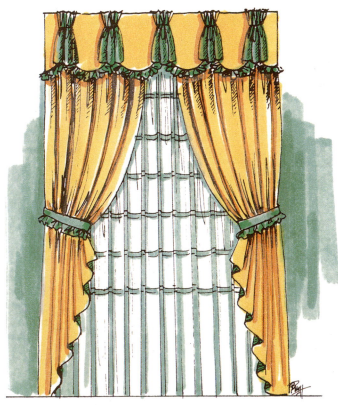

Tie-back Draperies with Austrian
Valance & Shade

Space Pleated Queen Ann Valance with
Scalloped Edge over Tie-backs & Sheers

Multiple Tie-backs over Cafe Curtains for a Warm Country Feeling

Pinch Pleated Drapery with Fringe

Ruffled Tie-backs with Bow & Rosettes over Pull-down Shade

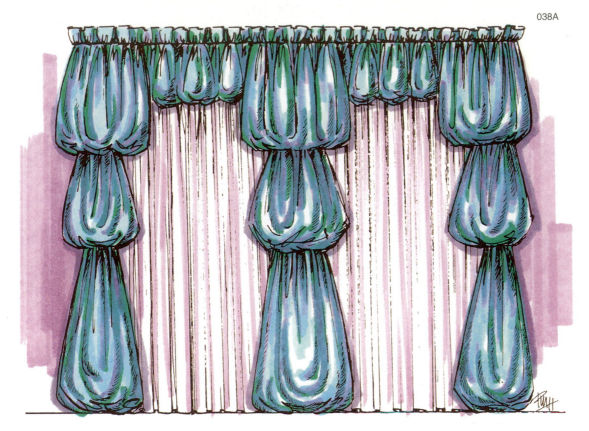

Rod Top Only Balloon Draperies

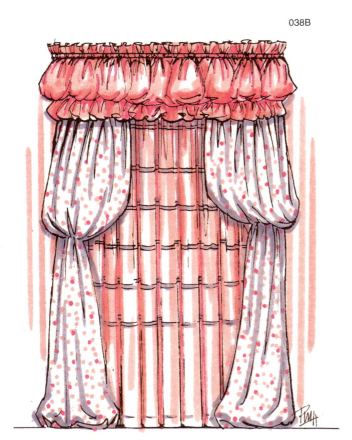

Double Rod Top Valance with
Puffed Tie-backs over Sheers

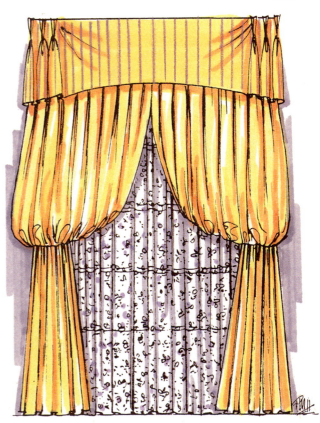

End-pleated Valance with Puffed Tie-backs
over Lace Curtain

VALANCES

039A

Open Kingston Valance on Dec. Rod

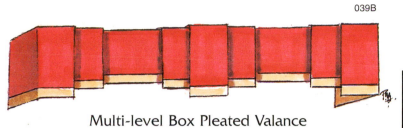

039B

Multi-level Box Pleated Valance

039C

Soft Cornice with Banners

039D

Banner Valance

039E

Scalloped Tabbed Valance with Trim

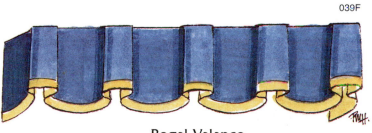

039F

Regal Valance

040A

Arched & Gathered Valance with Rope

040B

Box Pleated Valance with Tabs

040C

Gathered Handkerchief Valance

040D

Queen Ann Valance

040E

Tear Drop Valance

041A

Arched Valance with Bows
Gathered on Rod

041B

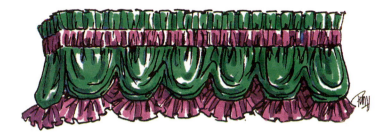

Cloud Valance with Stand-up Ruffle

041C

Empire Valance with Jabots

041D

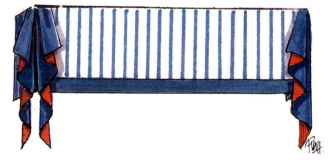

Plain Banded Valance with Jabots

041E

Tab-top Valance on Dec. Rod

042A

Rod Pocket Multiple Arched Valance

042B

Rolled Stagecoach Valance
with Wide Knotted Tie Bands

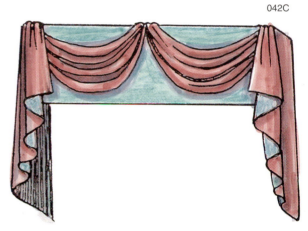

042C

Swags & Jabots over Soft Cornice

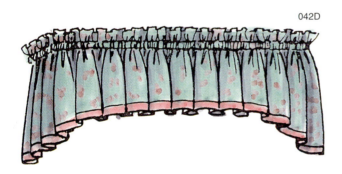

042D

Rod Pocket Arched Valance

042E

Gathered Valance on Top & Bottom Rods
with Multiple Bow Ties

42

043A

Multiple Point Valance with Edge Banding

043B

Box Pleated Valance with Twisted Cording

043C

Triple Cone Pleated Valance on Dec Rod

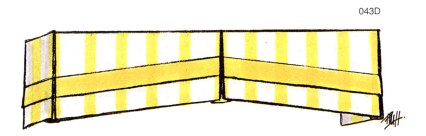

043D

Tapered Box Pleated Valance with Banding

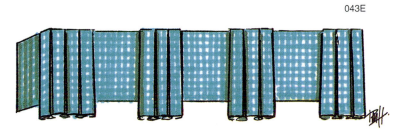

043E

Valance with Triple Box Pleats

Swags & Cascades over
Lambrequin Valance

Balloon Shade with Double Knotted Cords

Shaped Valance with Triple Knots

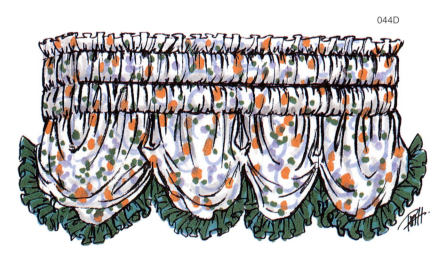

Cloud Valance with Ruffles
on Double Flat Rods

045A

Gathered Valance under Narrow Cornice
with Bows at Corners

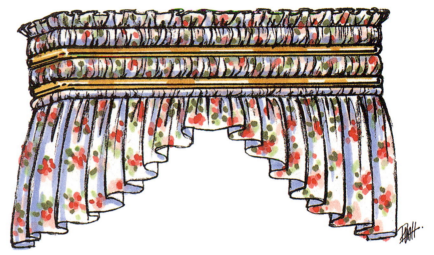

045B

Gathered Valance with Dec Rods Between
& Arched Ruffle Below

045C

Triple 4½″ Gathered Flat Rod Valance

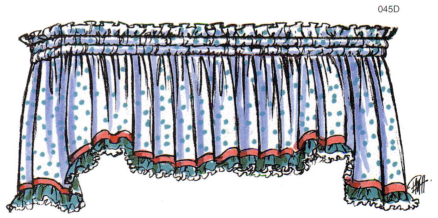

045D

Arched Gathered Valance with Ruffles
on Narrow Double Rods

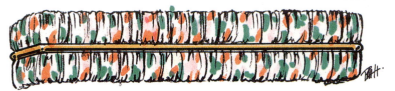

046A

Two Gathered Valances on Flat Rods
with Dec Rod in Middle

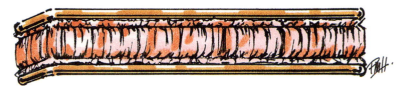

046B

Gathered Valance on Flat Rod
with Dec Rods at Top & Bottom

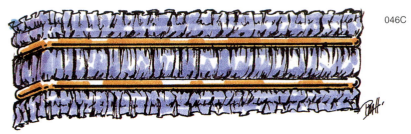

046C

Gathered Valance with Flat Rod in Middle
& Two Dec Rods Between

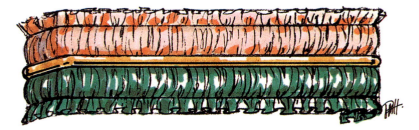

046D

Two 4½″ Flat Rods with Dec Rod in Middle

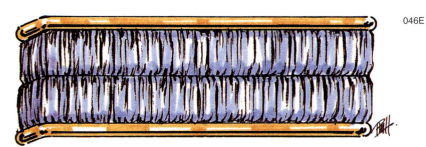

046E

Two 4½″ Flat Rods with
Dec Rods Top & Bottom

Double Pinch Pleat

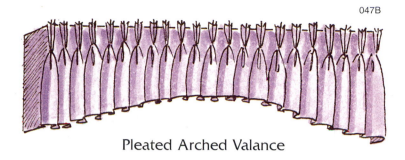

Pleated Arched Valance

French Pleated Valance

Double Pleat Queen Ann

Spaced Pleated Valance

Queen Ann Valance

Kingston Valance

Space Pleated Queen Ann Valance

RTO Arched Valance

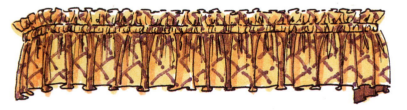

RTO Valance

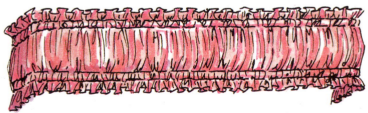

RTB Valance

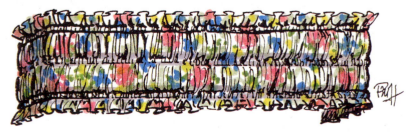

Double RTB Valance

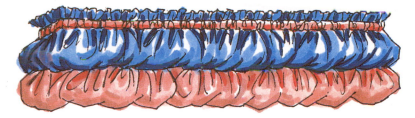

049A

Double RTB Valance

049B

RTB Valance with Lower Rod Lifted

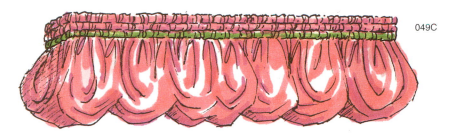

049C

Cloud Valance with Shirred Heading

049D

Cloud Valance with Rod Pocket Heading

049E

Cloud Valance with Standup Ruffle

049F

Balloon Valance with Piping

Rod Top Swag & Cascade
050A

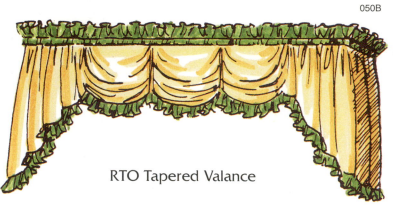

RTO Tapered Valance
050B

RTO Swag & Jabot Valance
050C

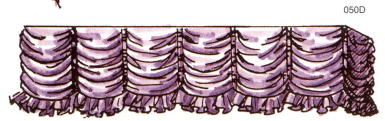

Austrian with Fringe
050D

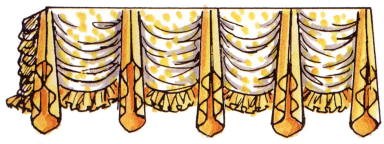

Austrian with Jabots
050E

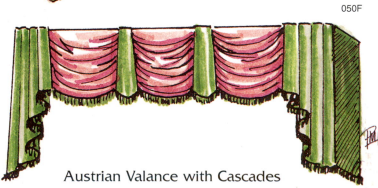

Austrian Valance with Cascades
050F

051A

Stagecoach Valance

051B

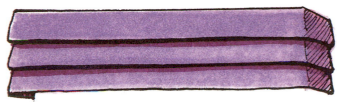

Mock Roman

051C

Scalloped Valance with Fringed Edge

051D

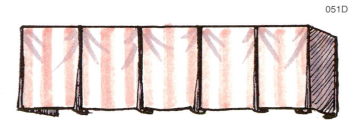

Inverted Box Pleat

051E

Inverted Box Pleat with Banding

051F

Box Pleat with Banding

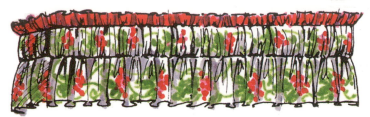

052A

Rod Pocket with Standup Ruffle

052B

Arched Rod Pocket

052C

Double Rod Pocket with
Standup Top & Bottom

052D

Double Rod Pocket with Standup

052E

Double Ruffled Valance Shirred on Rod

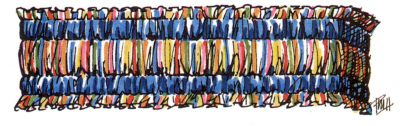

052F

Double Rod Pocket RTB with Standup

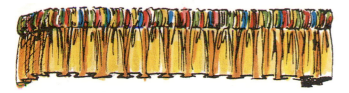

053A

Rod Pocket Heading with No Standup

053B

Double Rod Pocket with No Standup

053C

Double Rod Pocket Cloud Valance

053D

Triple Rod Pocket with Multiple Fabrics

053E

4" Shirred Heading

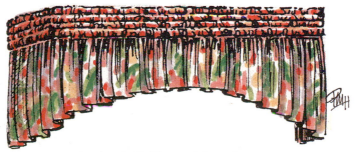

053F

Arched 4" Shirred Heading

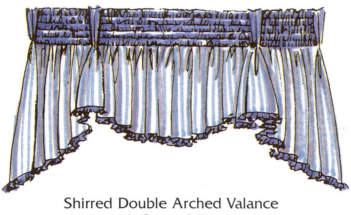

054A

Shirred Double Arched Valance
with Spaced Pleats

054B

Rod Pocket Spacer Valance

054C

Double Rod Pocket with Ruffles
& Tapered Sides

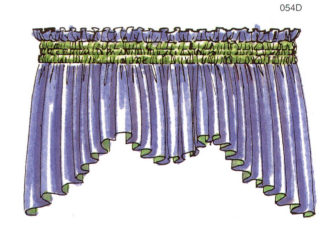

054D

Double Arched Valance with Shirred
Heading & Tapered Sides

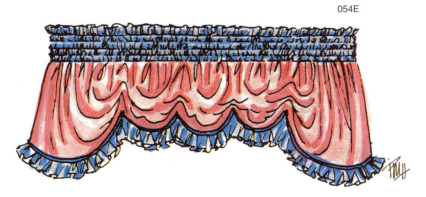

054E

Shirred Cloud Valance with Dropped Sides & Ruffle

055A

French Pleated Valance with
Tapered Sides

055B

Austrian Valance with
Side Cascades

055C

Rod Pocket Petticoat Valance

055D

New Orleans Valance with 6" Ruffle

055E

Rod Pocket Valance with Tapered Sides

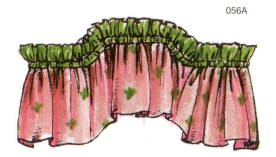

056A

Arched Valance

056B

Alternate – Traditional Swag

056C

Valance with Bows

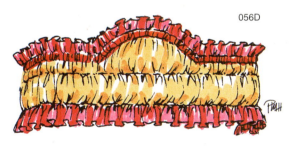

056D

Rod Pocket Valance with
Cathedral Top

056E

Double Arched Rod Pocket Valance

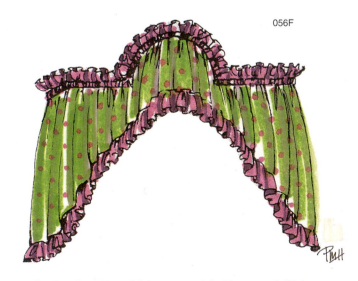

056F

Cathedral Top Valance with Tapered Sides

057A

057B

Swags & Cascades over Dec. Rod

Swags & Cascades with Ropes & Fringe

057D

057C

Turban Swags

Fabric Draped through Sconces

SWAGS, CASCADES & JABOTS

058A

Raised Swags over Tie-backs

058B

Sheer Swag with Knots

058C

Swags over Dec. Rod with Inverted Cascades

058D

Swag & Jabot with
Tassels & Rope

059A

**Single Swag & Cascades
with Rosettes**

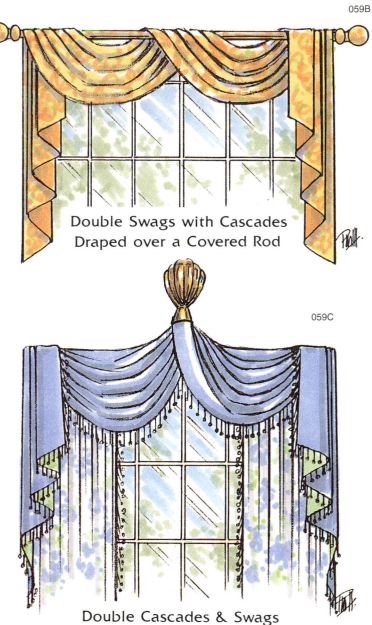

059B

**Double Swags with Cascades
Draped over a Covered Rod**

059C

**Double Cascades & Swags
Joined in the Middle**

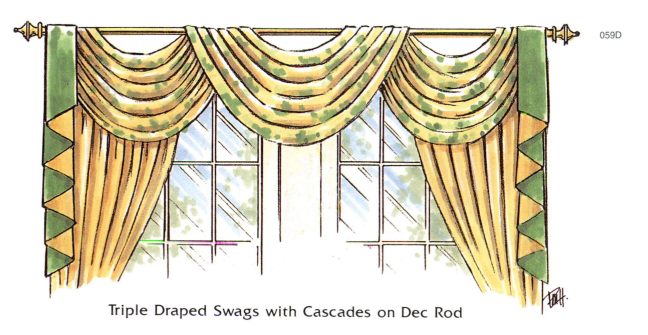

059D

Triple Draped Swags with Cascades on Dec Rod

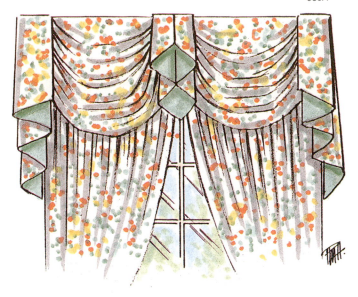

060A

Double Swag with Cascades

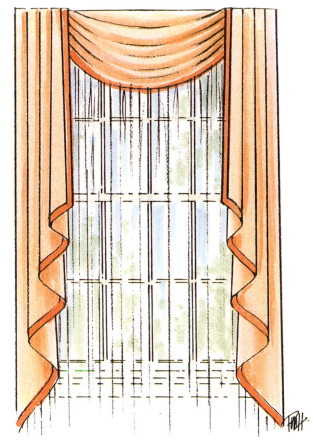

060B

Single Swag with Cascades

060C

Long Single Swag with
Two Tiers of Cascades

060D

Angled Double Swags
& Cascades with Rosettes

60

061A

**Double Swags with Ruffles
& Bows over Cascades**

061B

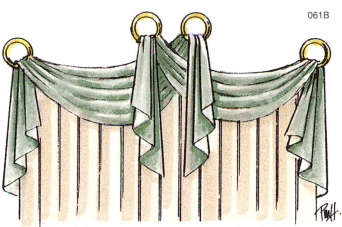

**Double Swags Crossed in Middle
with 4 Single Cascades on Rings**

061C

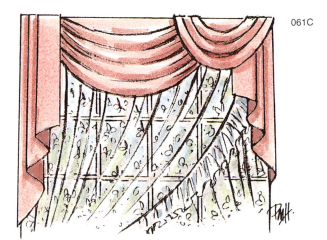

Asymetric Swags & Cascades

061D

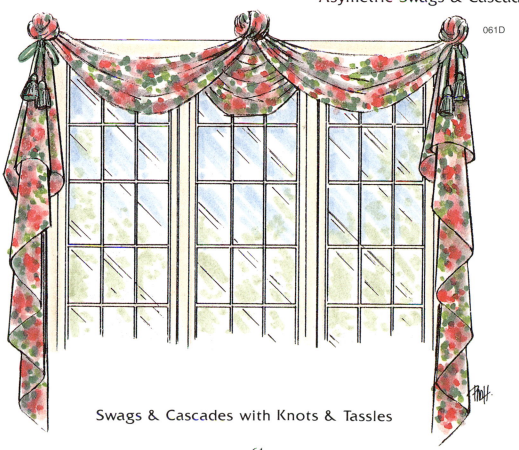

Swags & Cascades with Knots & Tassles

Formal Swags & Cascades

Swags & Rosettes & Center Jabot

Swag with Maltese Cross Ties

Gathered Swag

063A

Swag & Cascades with Ruffle
over Balloon Shade

063B

Draped Swag

063C

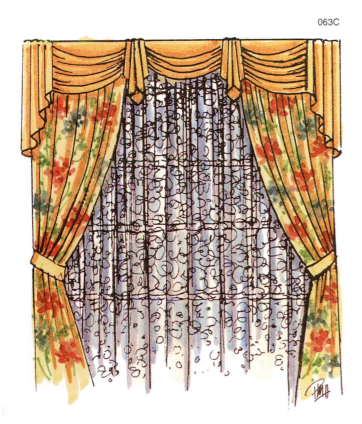

Swags & Jabots over Lace Panels

063D

Swag Draped over Rod

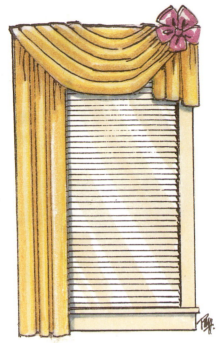

Swag with Rosette &
Asymmetric Cascades

Double Swag with Plain Cascades over Print

Swags & Long Cascades over French Doors

Swag & Cascade with Ties

Swag with Rosettes & Cascades

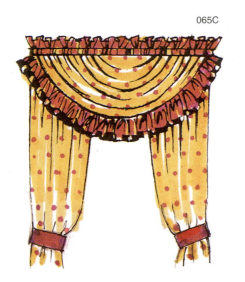

Ruffled Swag over Tie-backs

Double Swag with Rosettes & Cascades

Double Swag with Cascades & Pleated Edge

Ruffled Balloon Swag

066A

066B

066C

066D

066E

066F

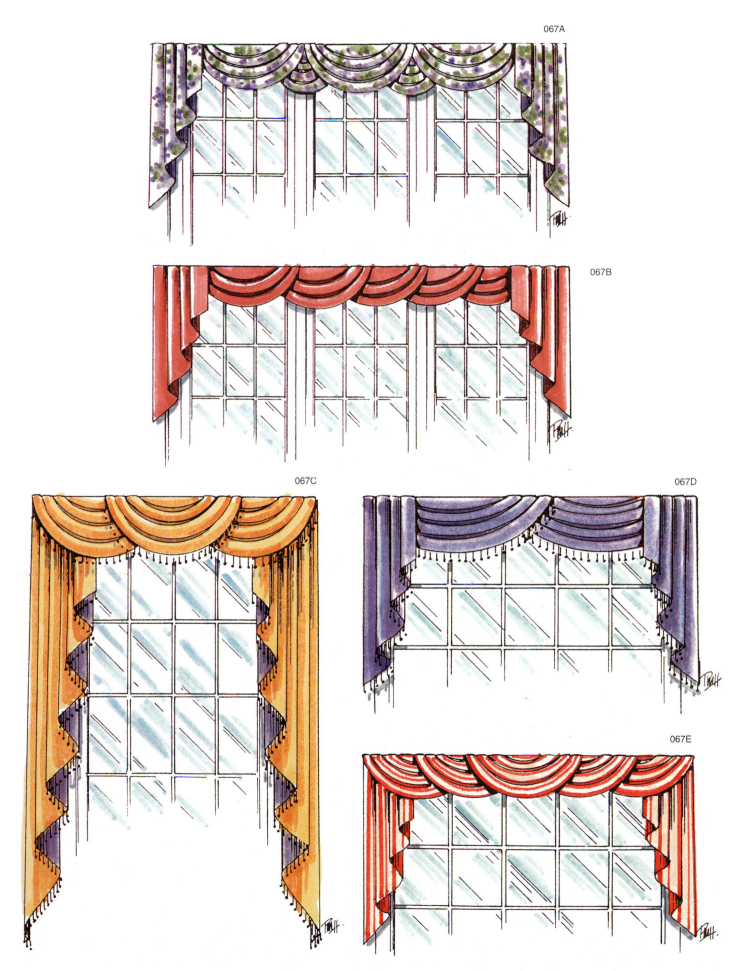

067A

067B

067C

067D

067E

SWAG & CASCADE TYPES

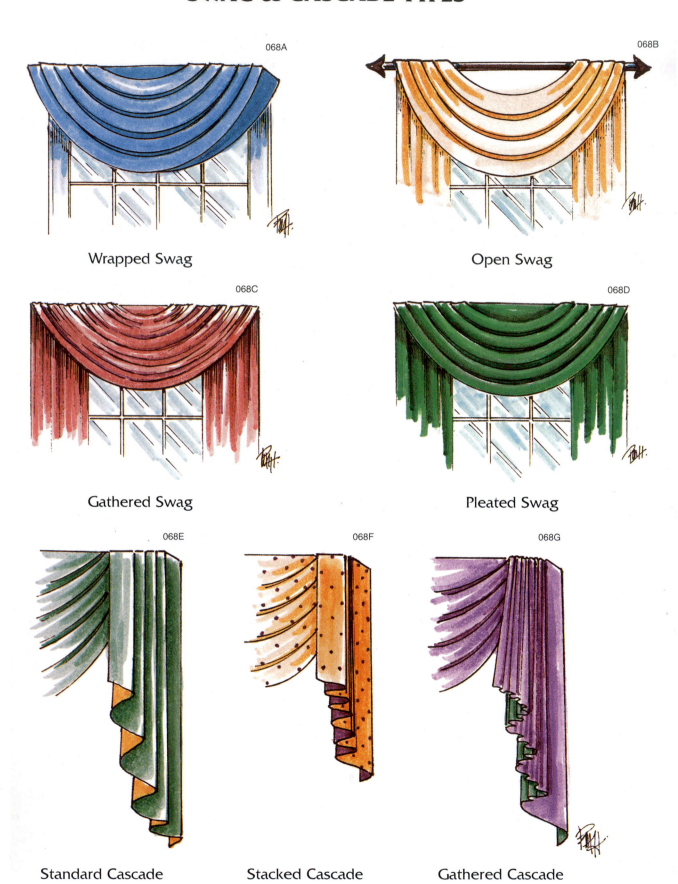

068A

Wrapped Swag

068B

Open Swag

068C

Gathered Swag

068D

Pleated Swag

068E

Standard Cascade

068F

Stacked Cascade

068G

Gathered Cascade

SWAGS & CASCADES
Yardage Requirements

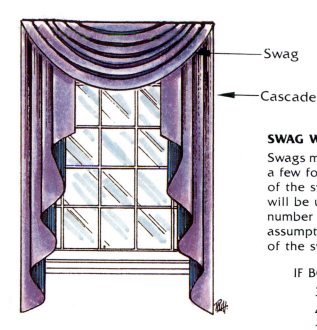

Swag

Cascade

Swags are top treatments or valances, used over draperies or blinds or sometImes alone. They are usually draped into soft, graceful folds, using fabrics that drape easily. It is more interesting to use an uneven number of swags. Swags should be lined.

Cascades are folded pieces of fabric that fall from the top of the drapery heading or valance to create a zig-zag effect. Cascades must be lined with the cover fabric or one that contrasts.

Yardage:
Swags — Based on an average of 44" per swag, you will need 2 yards of fabric per swag.

Cascades — Double the longest length, add 4" and divide by 36. This will give you the number of yards needed for a single pair of cascades.

SWAG WIDTH, BOARD FACE & NIMBER OF SWAGS

Swags may vary in width from 20" to over 70". Very small swags will have only a few folds. Extremely wide swags will have a limited drop length. The width of the swag is determined by the board face and the number of swags that will be used on each treatment. The following guide will help determine the number of swags needed based on the board face. The guide is based on the assumption that swag overlap will start approximately 1/2 or less the width of the swag face.

IF BOARD FACE IS:	NUMBER OF SWAGS NEEDED IS:
36" to 48"	1 swag
49" to 70"	2 swags
71" to 100"	3 swags
101" to 125"	4 swags
126" to 150"	5 swags
151" to 175"	6 swags
176" to 200"	7 swags
201" to 225"	8 swags
226" to 250"	9 swags
251" to 275"	10 swags
276" to 300"	11 swags

SWAG WIDTH:
To find the width of each swag, divide the board face width by one or more than the number of swags used and multiply by 2.

Example:
Board face width = 127"   Number of swags = 5
127" ÷ 6 = 21.16 × 2 = 42.33 or 43" width for each swag.

The standard drop lengths of swags are 16", 18", or 20". Usually 6 or 7 folds are placed across the top of a traditional swag with a standard drop. Swags that have shallow drops of 12" will have 3 or 4 folds.

The chart below is an average guide to help you in finding swag drop based on face width.

IF SWAG FACE WITH IS:	AVERAGE DROP WILL BE:
20"	10" to 13"
25"	12" to 17"
30"	14" to 19"
35"	14" to 20"
40"	14" to 21"
45"	16" to 23"
50"	16" to 23"
OVER 60"	18" to 24"

CASCADES & JABOTS

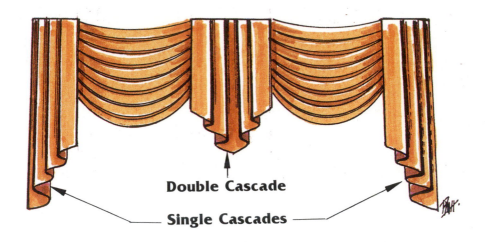

Double Cascade

Single Cascades

CASCADES

SINGLE TRADITIONAL CASCADE
(Yardage is for one cascade only)

Lined in contrasting fabric:
Length: *CL of face = FL (long point) plus 4" extra
         CL of lining = FL (long point) plus 4 " extra
Width: Allow one width for face & one width for lining

Self lined:
Length: FL (long point) × 2 plus 4" = CL of face & lining
Width: One width will accomodate face & lining

DOUBLE CASCADE
Length: Contrast or self lined — FL plus 4" = CL
Width: (face) — one width per Double Cascade (up to 14")
       (lining) — one width per Double Cascade

Note: *CL = cut length   FL = Finished Length

JABOTS

Jabots are decorative pieces of fabric that are hung over seams
or between swags on a valance. Jabots may be tie
shaped, cone shaped, or rounded on the bottom.

Yardage: Allow approximately one third yard of fabric for each jabot.

EMPIRE SWAG WITH JABOTS

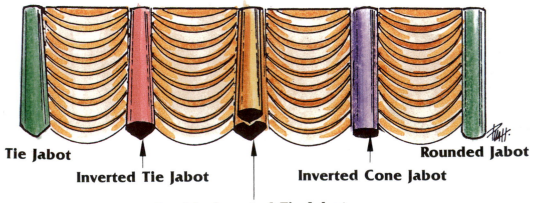

Tie Jabot

Inverted Tie Jabot

Double Inverted Tie Jabot

Inverted Cone Jabot

Rounded Jabot

CORNICE BOXES, LAMBREQUINS, ETC.

Cornice Box with Gold-Leaf Heading & Ties

Cornice Box with Gathered Panels

Soft Cornice with Swags & Cascades

Arched Cornice Box with Knotted Swag

CORNICE BOXES, LAMBREQUINS, ETC.

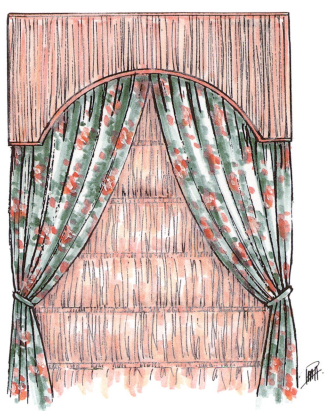

Shirred Cornice over Tie-backs

Lambrequin with Welt Edge
over Roman Shade

Shirred Lambrequin over
Pleated Drapery

Cornice Box with Shirred
Band & Ruffled Cascade

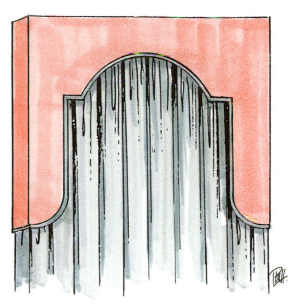

Shaped Cornice Box with
Vertical Side Drops

Bottom Banded Cornice Box
with Matching Draperies

Button Swagged Cornice

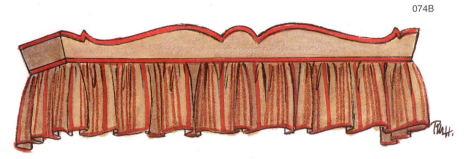

Shaped Crown Cornice with Gathered Valance

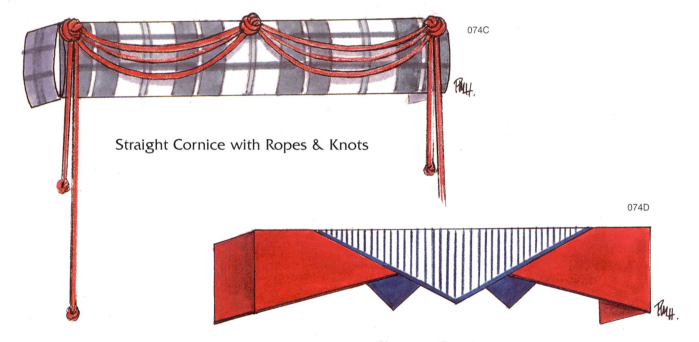

Straight Cornice with Ropes & Knots

Chevron Cornice

Pagoda Cornice with Long Fringe

075A

Shaped Cornice with Large Tassels

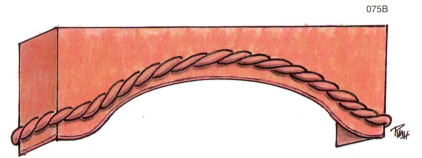

075B

Arched Cornice with Twisted Rope

075C

Shaped Cornice with Fringe

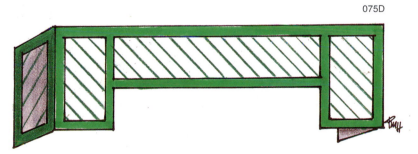

075D

Box Shaped Cornice with Long Side Drops

075E

Multi-Fabric Cornice

Sunburst Cornice

Pagoda Cornice

Straight Cornice with Shaped Crown

Custom Shaped Cornice

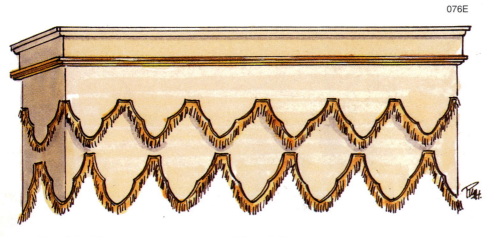

Double Fringe Cornice with Wood Crown

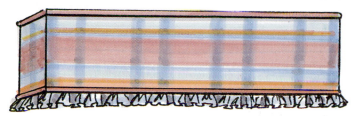

077A

Cornice Box with Ruffle on Bottom

077B

Cornice Box with Swag & Rosettes

077C

Cornice Box with Shirred & Flat Panels

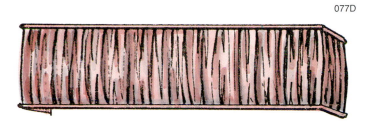

077D

Shirred Cornice Box

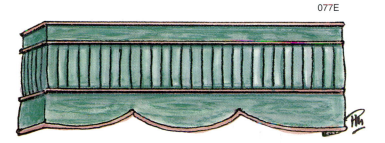

077E

Cornice Box with Pleated Fabric in Middle

078A

Real Wood Cornice with Painted Leaf Design

078B

Cornice with Real Wood Header

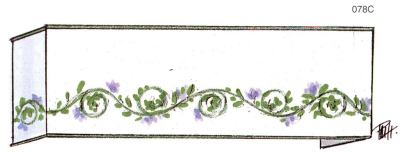

078C

Straight Cornice with Stenciled Design

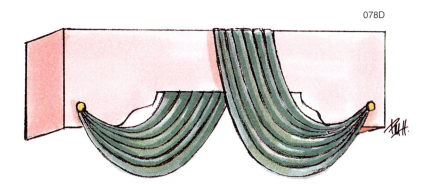

078D

Cornice with In-and-out Swag

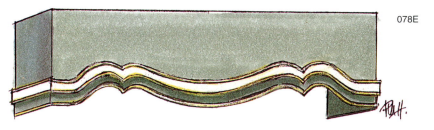

078E

Cornice with Shaped & Raised Banding

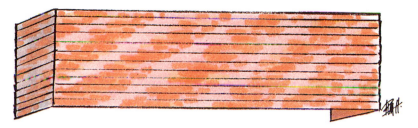

079A

Cornice with Honeycomb Pleating

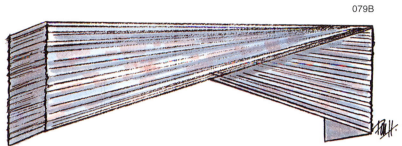

079B

Cornice with Diagonally Arched Pleating

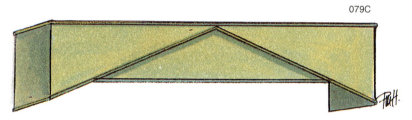

079C

Cornice with Unique Angled Top & Welting

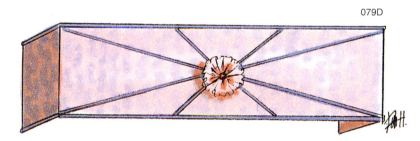

079D

Straight Cornice with Diagonal Welts
& Center Rosette

079E

Cornice with Rounded Gathered Top
& Large Scalloped Bottom

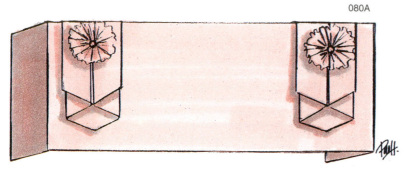

080A

Straight Cornice with Rosettes & Jabots

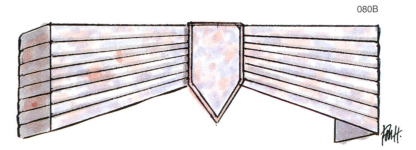

080B

Pleated Arched Cornice with Special Center Piece

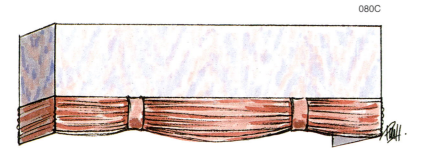

080C

Cornice with Unique Pleated Bottom

080D

Straight Cornice with Gathered Hourglass & Rosette

080E

Cornice with Center Jabot

081A

Cornice Box with
Shirred Bottom Band

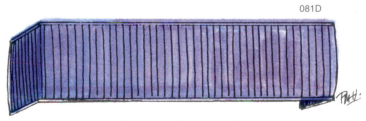

081B

Cornice Box with
Special Welting

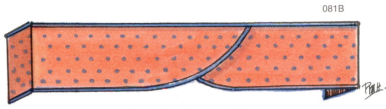

081C

Scalloped Bottom
with Banding

081D

Cornice Box with
1" Pleats

081E

Cornice Box with
Fabric Insert

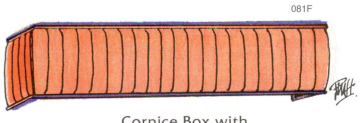

081F

Cornice Box with
2" Pleats

CORNICE BOX SHAPES

082A

082B

082C

082D

082E

082F

082G

082H

082I

082J

082K

082L

083A

083B

083C

083D

083E

083F

083G

083H

083I

083J

083K

083L

084A

084B

084C

084D

084E

084F

084G

084H

084I

084J

084K

084L

LAMBREQUINS & CANTONNIERES

085B

085A

085C

085E

085D

085F

085H

085G

085I

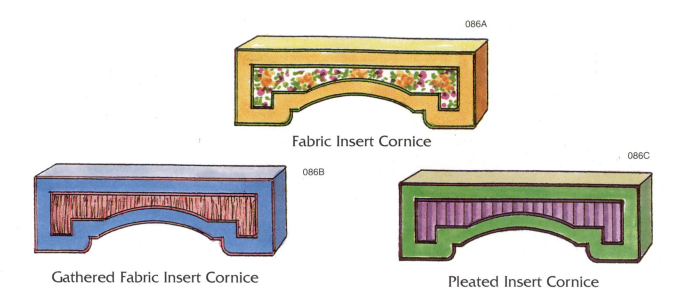

Fabric Insert Cornice

Gathered Fabric Insert Cornice

Pleated Insert Cornice

General Information

The cornices are padded with polyester fiberfill and constructed of wood.

Non-directional and solid fabrics should be railroaded to eliminate seams. Matching welting is standard on all cornices and is applied to the top and bottom edges. Coordinating colors for welting has a more dramatic effect.

When ordering cornices to fit tight applications (i.e. wall to wall, bay windows), be sure to measure at the elevation of this installation. "Exact outside face measurement - wall to wall installation". Allow 1″ for clearance.

Measuring:

Measure drapery rod from end bracket to end bracket and add four inches for rod clearance and cornice returns. Six (6″) returns are needed when mounted over a single rod and eight (8″) returns when mounted over a double rod.

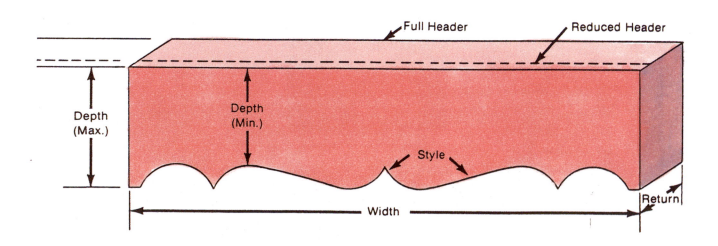

FABRIC SHADES

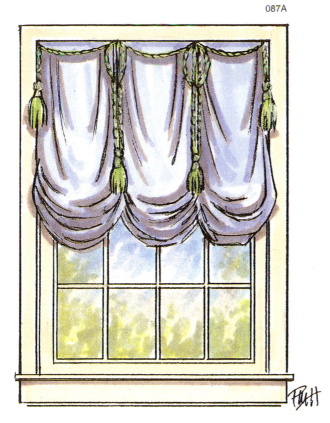

Balloon Shade with Rope Tassels

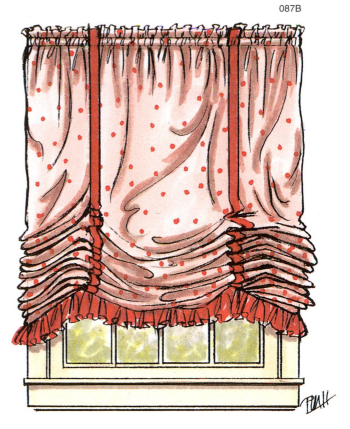

Suspender Balloon Shade

Double Rod Pocket Cloud Shade
with Bottom Ruffle

Specialty Soft Shade

FABRIC SHADES

088A

Stagecoach Shade with Ties

088B

Wide Pleated Balloon Shade

088C

Designer Cloud Shade

088D

Wide Cloud, Cloud Shade

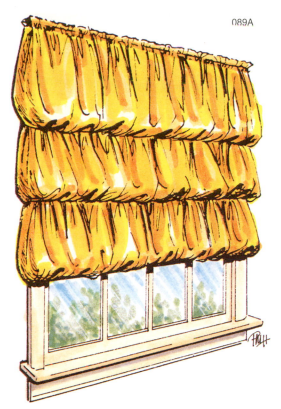

089A

Tiered Cloud Shade

089B

Cloud Shade with Optional
Ruffled Bottom

089C

Arched Top Cloud Shade

089D

Bottom Arched Balloon Shade

090A

Cloud Shade Gathered on a Pole
with Ruffle at the Top

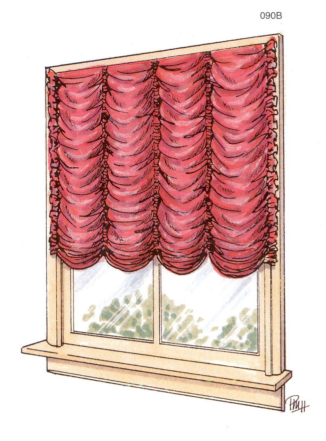

090B

Triple Fullness Fabric in Softly Scalloped Panels
Distinguish the Austrian Shade

090C

Cloud Shade with 4" Shirring
at Top to Give a Smocked Look

090D

Shirred Cloud Shade with Matching Valance

091A

Inverted Pleats and a Pouffed Bottom Edge
Characterize the Elegant Balloon Shade

091B

Pleated Balloon Shade with
Matching Valance

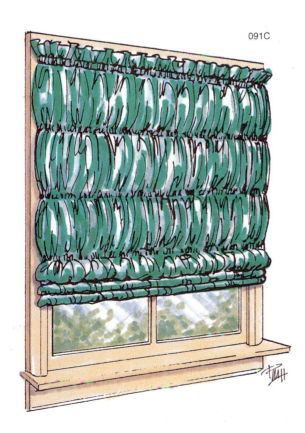

091C

Fabric Gathered Triple Fullness on Horizontal
Rods for a Full, but Tailored Look

091D

Rod Pocket Swagged Balloon Shade
over Mini Blind

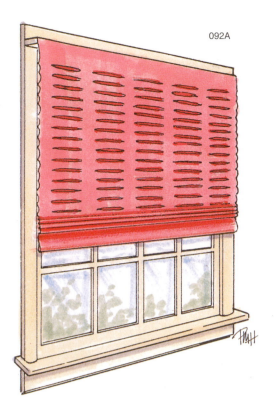

The Dramatic Accordion Look is
Created by Rows of Mini-pleats

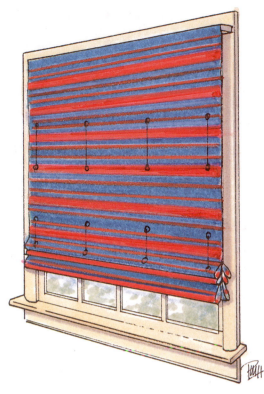

Brass Grommets and Front Cording Give
a Nautical Look to this Shade

A Flat, Simple Roman Shade that Draws
Up into Graceful Folds when Raised

A Cord at Each Edge Gives Needed
Support to this Bottom-up Shade

093A

Distinctive Horizontal Pleating Makes this
a Very Popular and Versatile Roman Shade

093B

Alternate Groups of Mini-pleats with Single Panels
Gives this Blind a Striking Look all its Own

093C

Soft Overlapping Folds Create a Cascading
Effect in this Roman Shade

093D

Alternating Large and Small Pleats form a
Repeating Pattern on this Roman Shade

094A

This Valance has Soft Folds
& No Returns

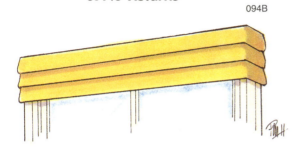
094B

For a More Finished Look, Soft Folds Wrap
Around the Sides of this Roman Valance

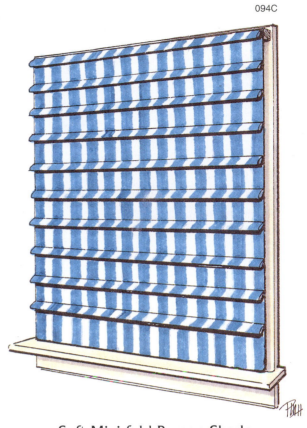
094C

Soft Mini-fold Roman Shade

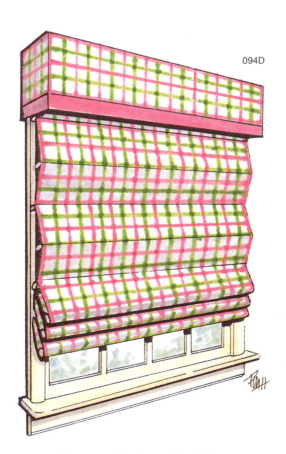
094D

Roman Shade with Valance
Overlapping

094E

This Very Simple Roman Shade is Flat
when Down & Draws Up in Graceful
Folds when Raised

CURTAINS & HEADING STYLES

Tabbed Curtain over Shutters

Tabbed Curtain gathered in Middle

Chevron Valance over Cafe Curtains

Curtain on Dec. Rod with Holdback

CURTAINS & HEADING STYLES

096A

Bow-tied Ruffled Tie-backs

096B

Tab-top Curtains on Dec. Rod

096C

Ruffled Tie-backs over Balloon Shade

Tab Top Curtains on Dec. Rod

Arched Rod Pocket Valance
over Straight Curtains

Ruffled Tie-backs over Shutters

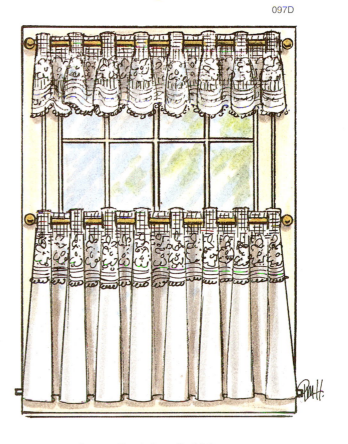

Lace Curtains & Valance
Threaded on Rod

Banded Tie-back Curtains

Banded Valance over Tie-backs

Tab Top Banded Curtains Tied-back

Tiered Curtains with Ribbon Banding

Sheer Lace tied-back Curtains
with Gathered Valance

Shirred Cafe Curtain on High Rod

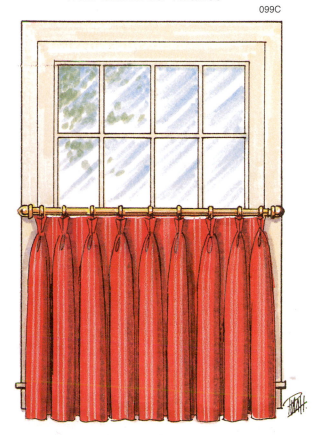

Cafe Curtains with French Pleated
Tops on Rings

Scalloped Valance over
Cafe Curtains

Priscilla Curtains with Ruffles

Valance on Brass Dec. Rod over
Tied-back Curtains with Ruffles

Rod Top Curtains with High Ties
and Large Ruffles

Priscilla Curtains with Rod Pocket Top

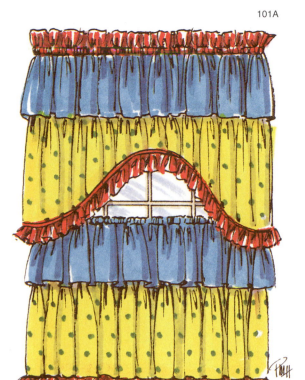

Cafe Curtains with Arched Top & Valance

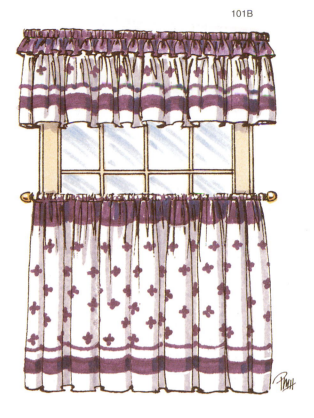

Cafe Curtains on Brass Rod with
Gathered Valance

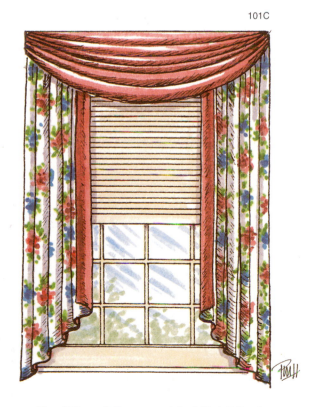

Traditional Swag with Mini Blind

Pleated Tab Top Cafe Curtains
on Brass Rod

Cafe Curtains Shirred Top-to-Bottom
Between Two Rods

Tied-back Curtains Gathered on Rod

Drapery Gathered on a Dec. Rod &
Tied-back with Large Bows

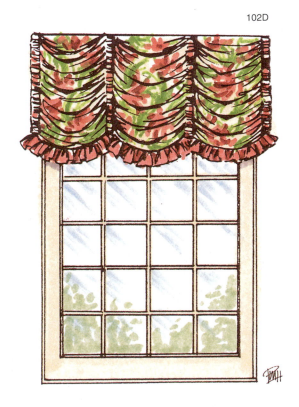

Austrian Shade with Ruffles

VARIOUS HEADING STYLES

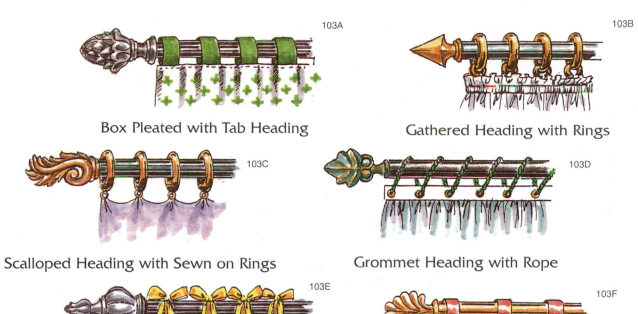

Box Pleated with Tab Heading

Gathered Heading with Rings

Scalloped Heading with Sewn on Rings

Grommet Heading with Rope

Scalloped Heading with Ties

Scalloped & Tabbed Heading

Tab-tied Curtains on Brass Dec. Rod

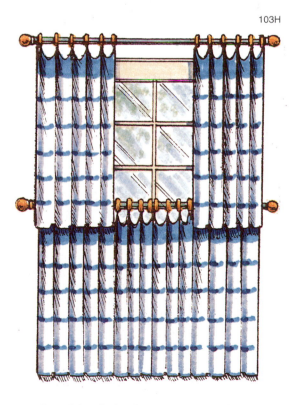

Double Cafe Curtains with Scalloped
Top on Brass Rod

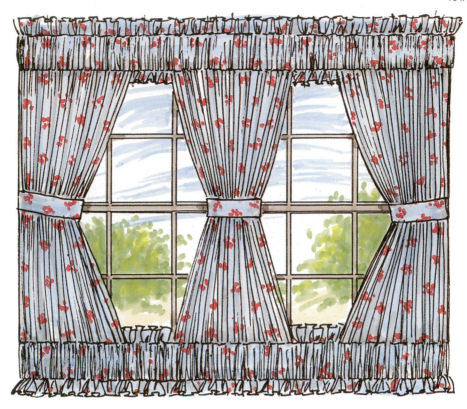

Rod Top & Bottom Curtain with Ties
and Center Sleeve

Rod Pocket Curtain with Tie-backs
and Center Sleeve

ACCESSORIES, TIE-BANDS, R.T.B.'S

105A

Straight Plain

105B
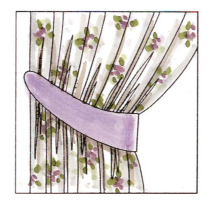
Tapered Plain

105C

Straight with Banding

105D
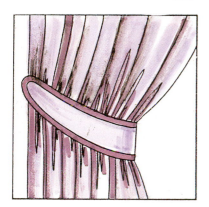
Tapered with Weld Cord

105E
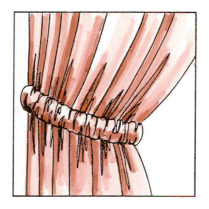
Shirred Jumbo Welt Cord

105F
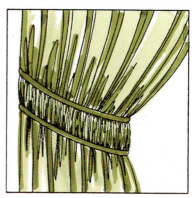
Straight Shirred with
Welt Cord

105G
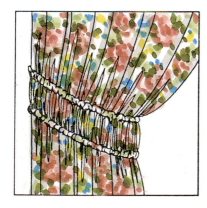
Straight Shirred

105H

Braided

105I
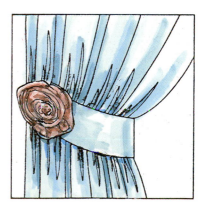
Straight with Rosette

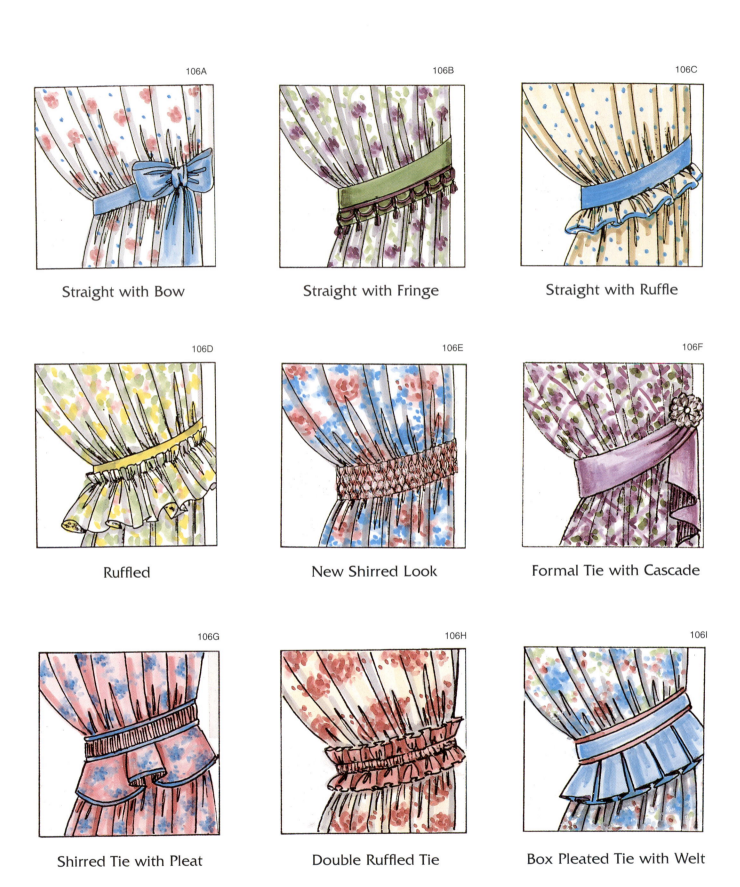

Straight with Bow

Straight with Fringe

Straight with Ruffle

Ruffled

New Shirred Look

Formal Tie with Cascade

Shirred Tie with Pleat

Double Ruffled Tie

Box Pleated Tie with Welt

ROUND TABLE COVERS

107A

Ruffled Overlay & Skirt with Tassles

107B

Round Overlay Tied with Bows

107C

Plain Round Cover — Lined or Unlined

107D

Plain Round Cover with Welt Edge

107E

Lace Square over Skirt

107F

Round Cover with Austrian Shirring

THROW PILLOWS

108A
Turkish Corners

108B
3" Ruffle with Welt

108C
Knife Edge with 1/4" Welt

108D
Shirred Welt

108E
Square Knot

108F
Heart Shaped with Ruffle

108G
Round Pillow with Welt & Ruffle

108H
Square Pillow with Plain Welt & Button

108I
Round Pillow with Plain Welt & Button

108J
Rope Welt on Knife Edge

108K
Tassled Corners

108L
Scalloped Ruffle with Welt Edge

PILLOWS & CUSHIONS

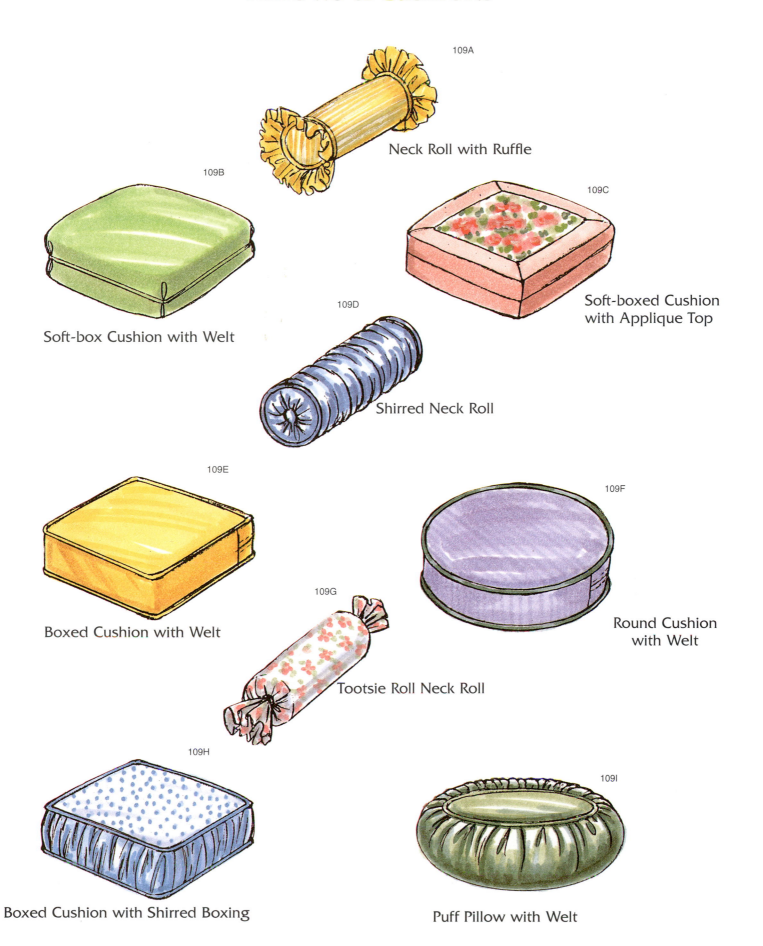

109A
Neck Roll with Ruffle

109B
Soft-box Cushion with Welt

109C
Soft-boxed Cushion
with Applique Top

109D
Shirred Neck Roll

109E
Boxed Cushion with Welt

109F
Round Cushion
with Welt

109G
Tootsie Roll Neck Roll

109H
Boxed Cushion with Shirred Boxing

109I
Puff Pillow with Welt

ACCESSORIES

110A

110B

Seat Cushions

Placemats

110C

Lamp Shades

Napkins & Napkin Rings

110E

Rosettes

110D

Bows

110F

111A

111C

Round Ottoman

111B

Square Ottoman

Fabric Draped Vanity Table

111D

Slip-covered Chair

111E

111F

Fabric Draped Through Sconces

Fabric Covered Divider

111G

Fabric Covered
Wastebasket

111H

111I

Seat Cushion

Sconce

111

Sunburst

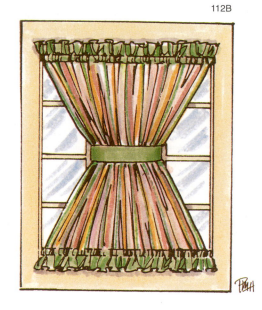

Hourglass Rod Top & Bottom

Diamond Rod Top & Bottom

Slant Rod Top & Bottom

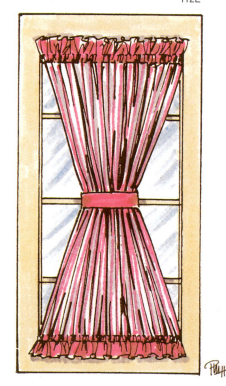

Hourglass Rod Top & Bottom

BED COVERINGS, BENCHES, HEADBOARDS

113A

Ceiling Mounted Valance over
Box Pleated Coverlet

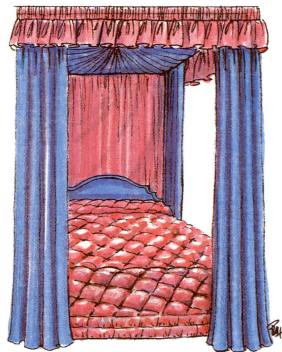

113B

Ceiling Mounted Rod Pocket Valance
over Quilted Bedspread

113C

Quilted Top Double Ruffled
Drop Bedspread

113D

Plain Bedspread with
Side Panels

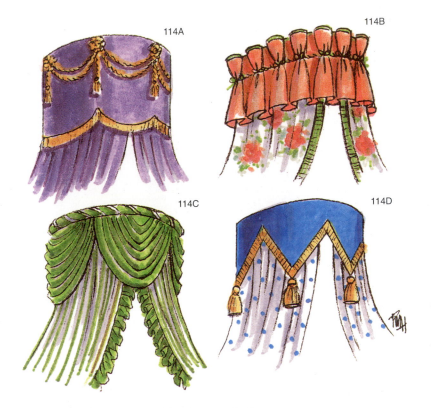

Various Bedspread Crowns

Rod Pocket Drapery with Dec. Rod
over Plain Bedspread

Swags & Cascades over Plain Bedspread
with Upholstered Headboard

Swags & Jabots with Maltese Cross Ties
over Plain Bedspread

115A

115B

Half-round Box Pleated Valance
with Draped Fabric held by Rosettes
Upholstered Headboard with Throw Spread

Fabric Draped over Decorative Pole
Coverlet with Tailored Dust Ruffle

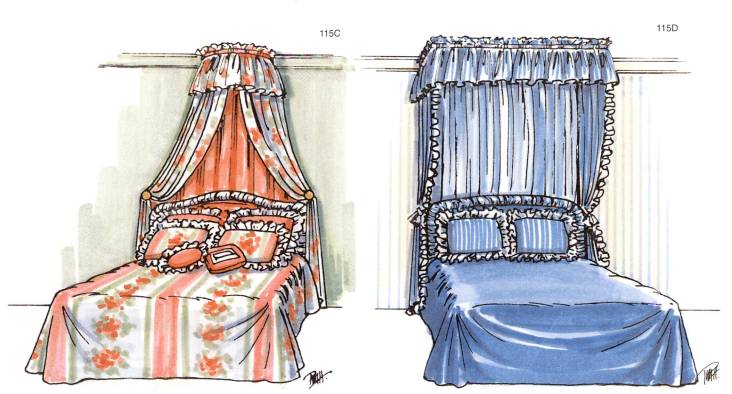

115C

115D

Half-round Ruffled Valance with
Fabric Draped over Hold Backs
Upholstered Headboard with Throw Spread

Rod Pocket Valance with Ruffled Tie-backs
Upholstered Headboard & Throw Spread

116A

Box Pleated Canopy Valance
   with Stationery Draperies

Quilted Coverlet over
   Box Pleated Dust Ruffle

116B

Gathered Canopy Valance
Ruffled Bedspread over Gathered Dust Ruffle

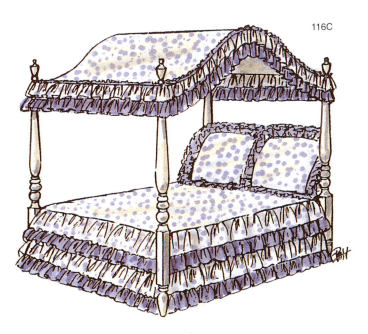

116C

Arched Canopy with Ruffles
Ruffled Bedspread & Dust Ruffle

116D

Gathered Canopy Valance over Tie Backs
Coverlet over Gathered Dust Ruffle

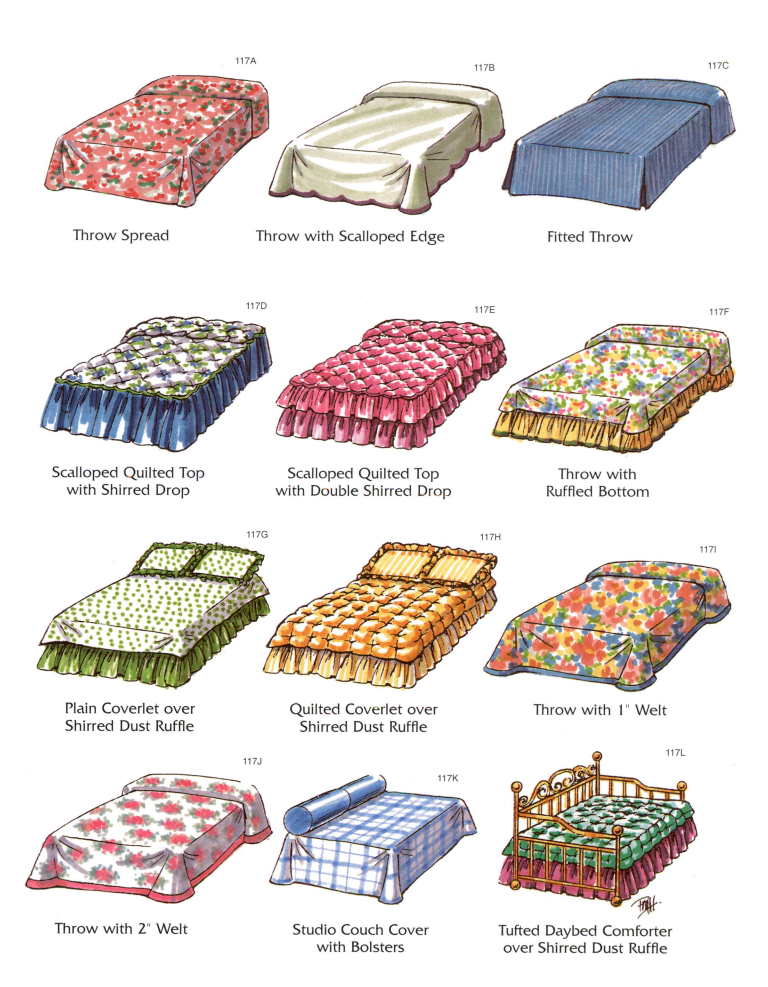

117A
Throw Spread

117B
Throw with Scalloped Edge

117C
Fitted Throw

117D
Scalloped Quilted Top
with Shirred Drop

117E
Scalloped Quilted Top
with Double Shirred Drop

117F
Throw with
Ruffled Bottom

117G
Plain Coverlet over
Shirred Dust Ruffle

117H
Quilted Coverlet over
Shirred Dust Ruffle

117I
Throw with 1" Welt

117J
Throw with 2" Welt

117K
Studio Couch Cover
with Bolsters

117L
Tufted Daybed Comforter
over Shirred Dust Ruffle

DUST RUFFLES

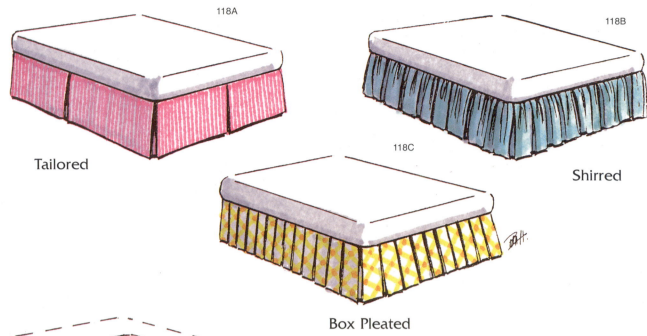

118A

Tailored

118B

Shirred

118C

Box Pleated

HOW TO MEASURE:
(Exact measurements are necessary)
A – Length of Boxsprings
B – Width of Boxsprings
C – Drop from top of Boxsprings to floor

UPHOLSTERED HEADBOARDS

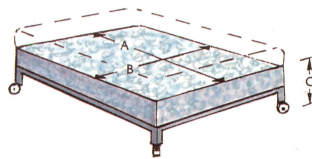

118D

118E

118F

118G

118H

118I

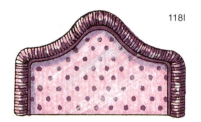

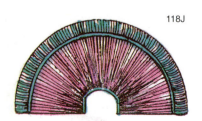

118J

DIMENSIONS

STYLE	TWIN	FULL	QUEEN	KING
D, I, F, G	41W X 51H	56W X 53H	62W X 55H	81W X 56H
J	41W X 53H	56W X 55H	62W X 57H	81W X 57H
E, H	41W X 49H	56W X 49H	62W X 51H	81W X 53H

UPHOLSTERED BENCHES

119A

Plain Covered Bench

119B

Covered Scalloped Bench

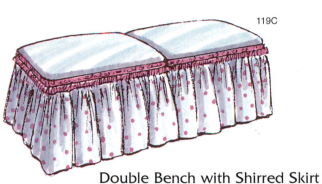

119C

Double Bench with Shirred Skirt

119D

Plain Bench with
Upholstered Legs & Top

PILLOW SHAMS

119E

Sham with 3" Ruffle

119F

Plain Sham with
1/4" Welt

119G

Quilted Sham with
2 1/2" Flange

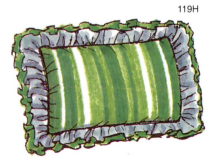

119H

Plain Sham with
Double Ruffle

119I

Sham with 1/4" Welt
and Ruffle

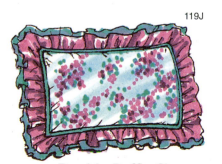

119J

Double Ruffle Sham
with 1/2" Welt

119K

Cylindrical Bolster
with Welt Trim

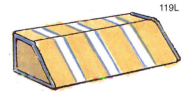

119L

Wedge Bolster with
Welt Trim

119M

Rectangular Bolster
with Welt Trim

YARDAGE SCHEDULE FOR BED COVERINGS

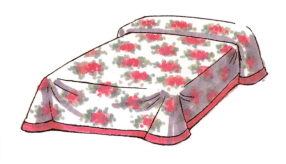

SPREADS

	36"	48"	54"
Twin	12 yards	8 yards	8 yards
Full	12 yards	12 yards	8 yards
Queen	15 yards	12 yards	12 yards
King	15 yards	12 yards	12 yards

Additional Yardage Requirements: For Prints—Add 1 yard
Additional Yardage Optional Features:
For Reverse Sham—Add 3 yards   For Jumbo Cord—Add 2 yards

COMFORTER YARDAGE

Twin, Full, Queen— 7 yards/side
King—11 yards/side

PILLOW SHAMS

1 1/2 yards—Ruffles Add 1 1/2 yards

DUSTERS

	36" Fabric		45" or Wider	
	Tailored	Shirred or 4" Box Pleat	Tailored	Shirred or 4" Box Pleat
Twin	3 3/4 yards	8 1/2 yards	2 3/4 yards	6 1/2 yards
Full	3 3/4 yards	8 1/2 yards	2 3/4 yards	7 yards
Queen	4 1/2 yards	10 yards	3 yards	7 1/2 yards
King	4 1/2 yards	10 yards	3 yards	7 1/2 yards

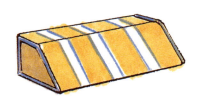

BOLSTERS

	36"	45"	54"
36"	1 1/2 yards	1 1/2 yards	1 yard
39"	2 yards	1 1/2 yards	1 yard
60"	2 yards	2 yards	2 yards
72"	2 1/2 yards	2 yards	2 yards

Add 1 Repeat of Pattern for Prints

GENERAL INFORMATION

Bedspreads are made to fit the following standard bed sizes:		Standard Drops:
Twin	39 x 75	Bedspreads 21"
Full	54 x 75	Coverlets 12"
Queen	60 x 80	Dusters 14"
King	72 x 84	Pillow Tuck 15"

121A

Rod Pocket Valance over Solid Wood Shutters

121B

Louvered & Solid Shutters with Valance

121C

Fabric Insert Shutters

121D

Draperies over Traditional Shutters

WOOD BLINDS & SHUTTERS

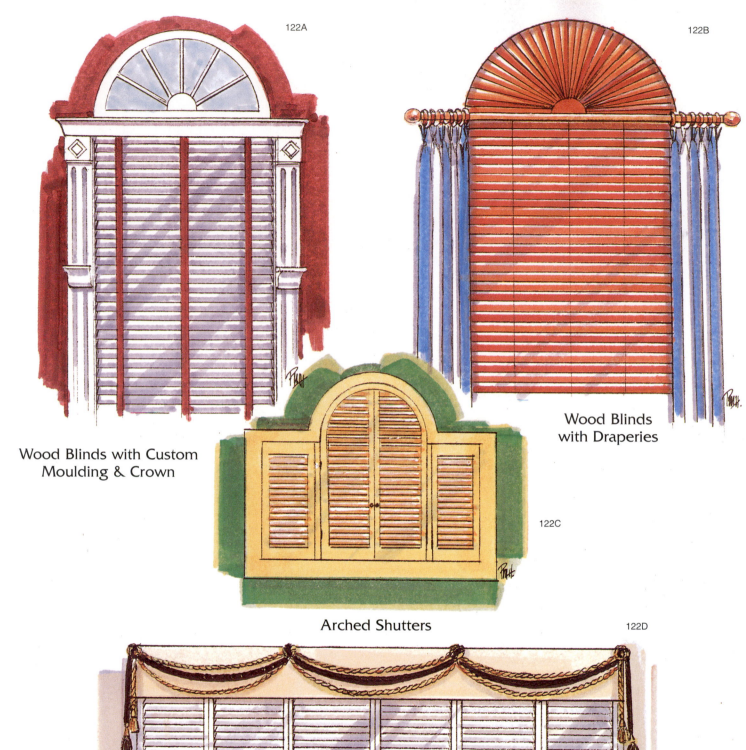

122A

Wood Blinds with Custom
Moulding & Crown

122B

Wood Blinds
with Draperies

122C

Arched Shutters

122D

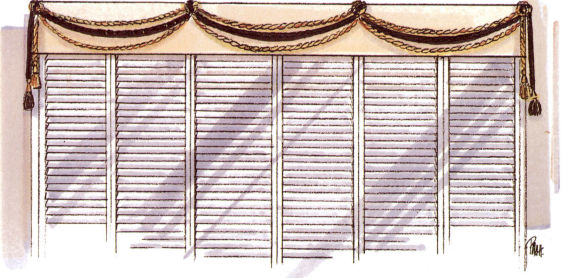

Cornice Box with Rope & Tassels over Shutters

Ruffled Swags Over Cafe Shutters

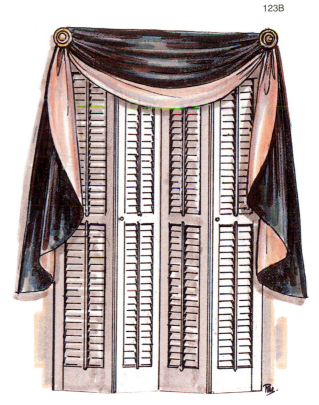

Two-tone Swag Over Full Shutters

Shutter With Shirred Fabric Insert

Gathered Valance Over Louvered Shutters

124A

Cornice Box Over White Wood
Blinds With Wide Tapes

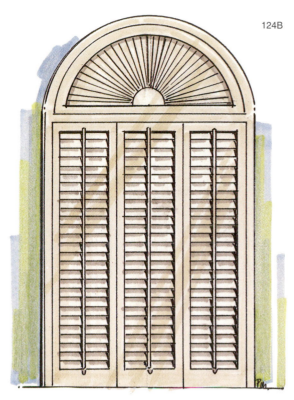

124B

Sunburst Shutter Over French Door Shutters

124C

Leaded Glass Over Wide Blade Shutters

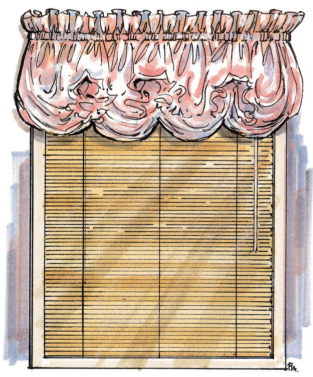

124D

1'' Wood Blind in Natural Finish
With Cloud Valance

**Cathedral Window with
Custom Fitted Shutters**

125B

**Shutters Custom Fitted to
Slanted Clerestory Window**

125C

**French Doors with Wood
Blinds & Chevron Valances**

125D

**Traditional Shutters
on Tall Window**

126A

Balloon Valance
over Wood Blind

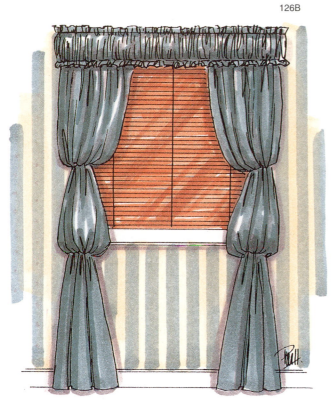

126B

Bishop Sleeve Draperies
over Wood Blind

126C

Fabric Swag with Side Drop
over Wood Blind

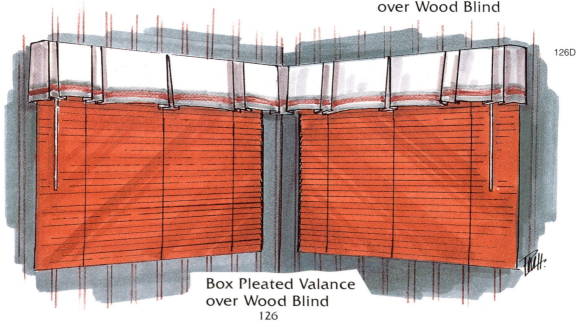

126D

Box Pleated Valance
over Wood Blind

Fabric Draped in Double
Swag

Lace Tie-backs over Wood Blinds

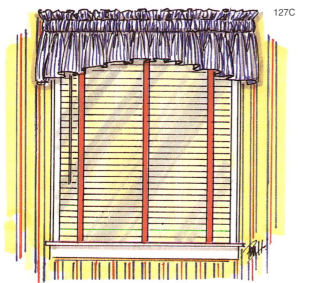

Arched Gathered Valance
over Wood Venetian Blind

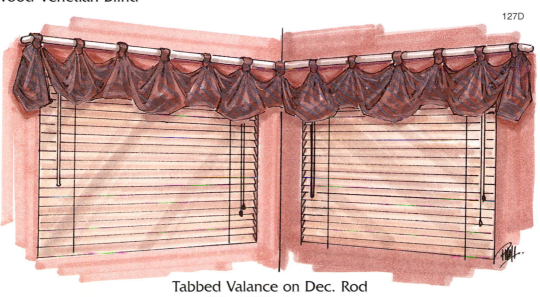

Tabbed Valance on Dec. Rod
over Wood Blind

128A

Swags & Jabots
over Half Shutters

128B

Shirred Valance with Ruffle over
Gathered Side Draperies & Wood Blind

128C

Bishop Sleeve Arched Valance
over Plantation Shutters

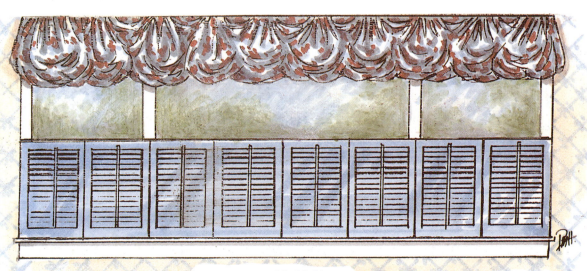

128D

Cloud Valance over Half Shutters

MINI-BLINDS, PLEATED SHADES, ROLLER SHADES

Drapery Folded over Dec. Rod over Pleated Shade

Fabric Draped over Pleated Shade

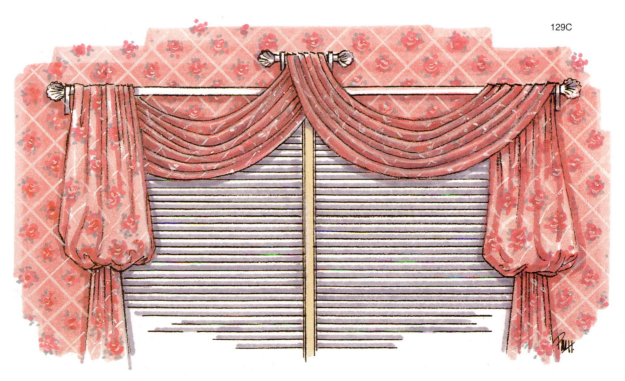

Fabric Draped over Pleated Shade

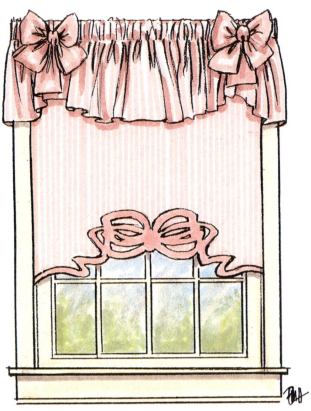

Gathered Valance with Bows over
Shade with Appliqued Bottom

Fringed Scalloped Roller Shade
with Valance

Banded Roller Shade with Valance

Rod Pocket Valance over Roller Shade

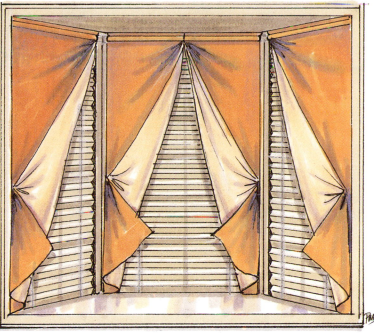

**Tab Curtains Tied Back
Over Roller Shade**

Flat Panels Pulled Back Over Pleated Shades

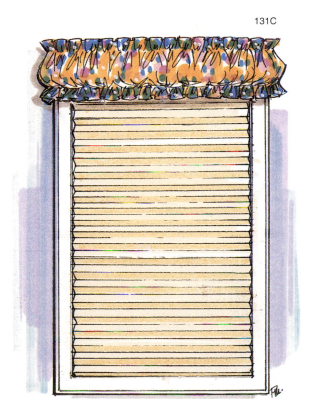

**Puffed and Ruffled Valance
Over Pleated Shade**

**Gathered Swag and Cascade
Over Pleated Shade**

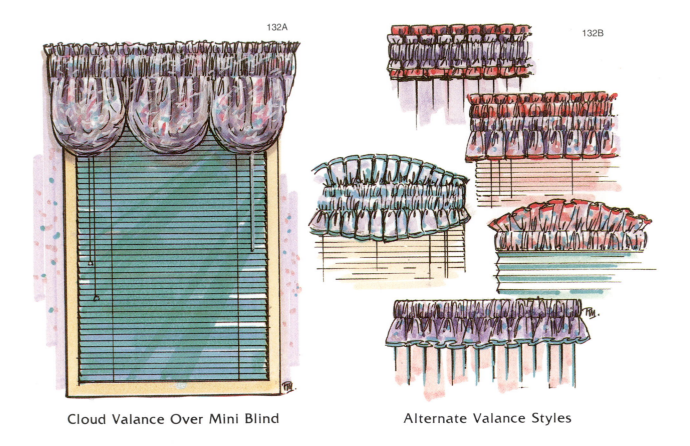

Cloud Valance Over Mini Blind

Alternate Valance Styles

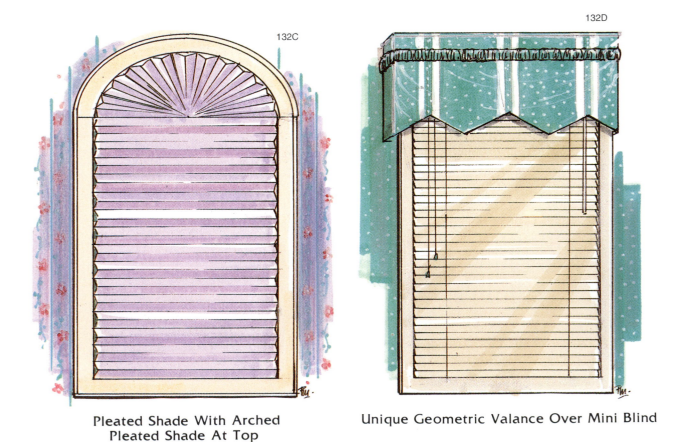

Pleated Shade With Arched
Pleated Shade At Top

Unique Geometric Valance Over Mini Blind

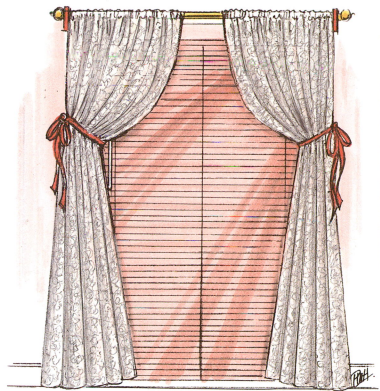

Lace Tie Backs on Dec Rod
over Mini Blind

Box Pleated Valance
over Pleated Shade

Scalloped Awning Valance
over Mini Blind

Full Gathered Valance
on Double Rods

134A

Handkerchief Tie over Pleated Blind

134B

Swag with Tassles & Fringe

134C

Cloud Shade with Ruffled Top & Tassles

134D

Short Swag on Dec Rod

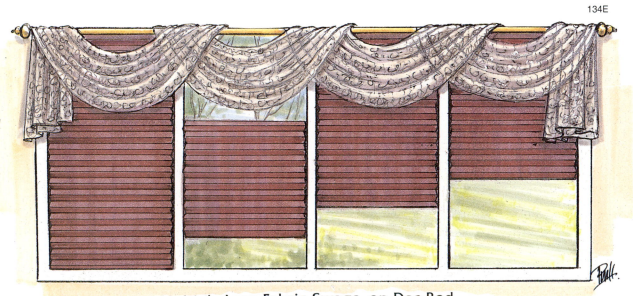

134E

Multiple Lace Fabric Swags on Dec Rod

135A

Simple Shirred Cornice Over Vertical Blinds

135B

Fabric or Wallpaper Inserts
Add a Designer Touch to Verticals

135C

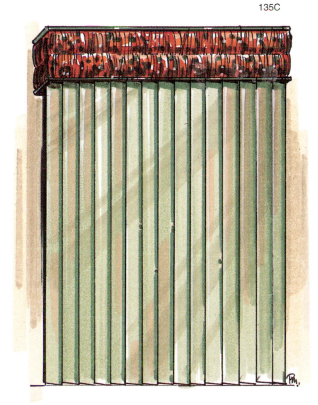

Double Gathered Cornice Over Vertical Blinds

135D

Vertical Blinds With Stagecoach Valance

VERTICALS

136A

Slant-top Vertical Blinds

136B

Vertical Blinds With Cornice Top

136C

Verticals Are A Great Solution To Bay Windows

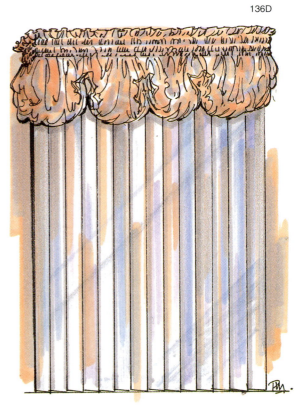

136D

Shirred Cloud Valance Adds
Softness to Vertical Blinds

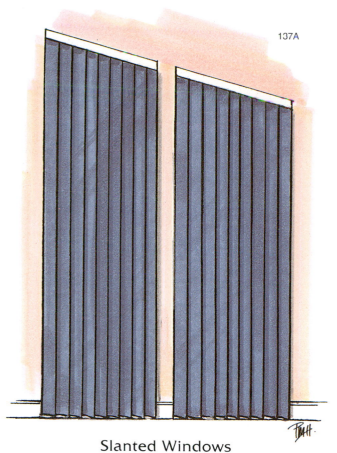

Slanted Windows
with Vertical Blinds

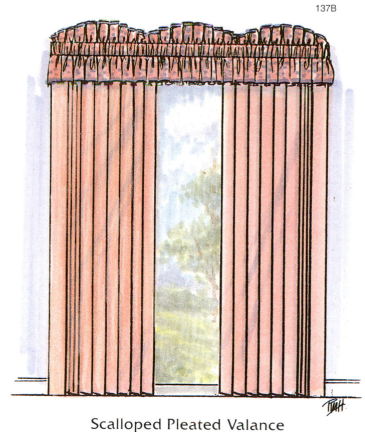

Scalloped Pleated Valance
over Vertical Blinds

Double Brass Rods over Vertical Blinds
with Brass Trim at Bottom

Decorative Stencil Design
on Vertical Blinds

**Swag with Ruffled Side Drops
over Vertical Blinds**

**Floor Length Fabric Swagged on
Shirred Rod over Vertical Blinds**

**Bay Window with Bishop Sleeve
Effect over Vertical Blinds**

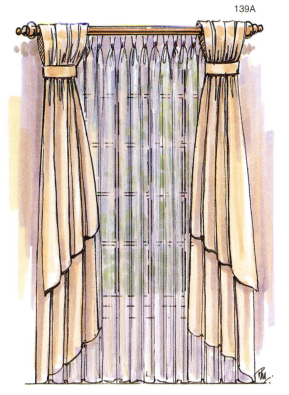

139A

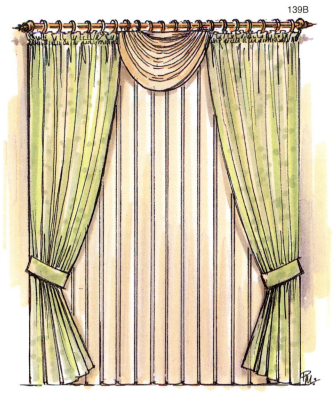

139B

Draperies Folded and Gathered Over Sheers

This Popular European Design Adds Elegance

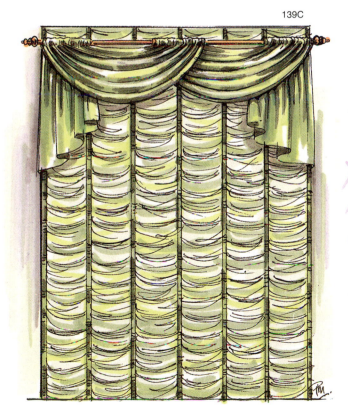

139C

139D

Another Unique European Style Valance

Kingston Valance With Ruffles and Border Top

POTPOURRI

Fabric Swagged Over Pole
With Cord and Tassle Trim

Two Large and One Small Swag
With Cascades

Arched Ruffled Sunburst and Tie Backs
Over Cafe Curtains

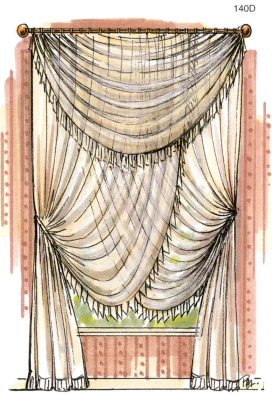

Deep Swag and Full Tie Backs are a
Popular European Style

Swagged Fabric with Cord Trim
over Asymetric Tie Back

Gathered Draperies Pulled
Back to Show Lining

Special Swag & Jabot Effect

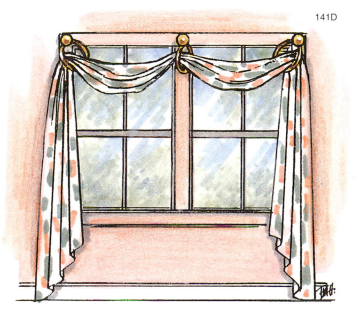

Fabric Swagged through
Large brass Rings

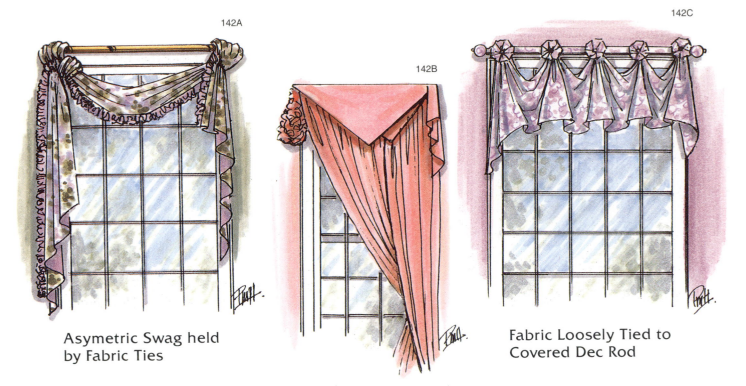

142A

Asymetric Swag held
by Fabric Ties

142B

Handkerchief Valance over
Asymetric Tie Back

142C

Fabric Loosely Tied to
Covered Dec Rod

142D

Draperies over Bay Window with
Large Swags held by Bows

143A

**Draped Swag with
Contrasting Lining**

143B

**Swag with Lifted Center
& Cascading Tails**

143C

Double Swagged Valance

143D

Single Swag with Rosettes

Swag with Asymetric Cascades

Boxed Swag Valance

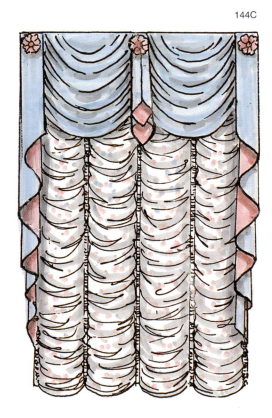

Swags Over Austrian Shade

Swag with Rosettes & Bow in Middle

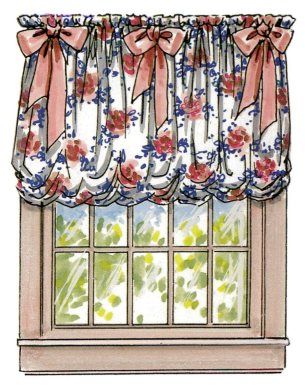

Cloud Shade with Bows at Top

Cloud Shade gathered on a pole
with ruffled upper edge

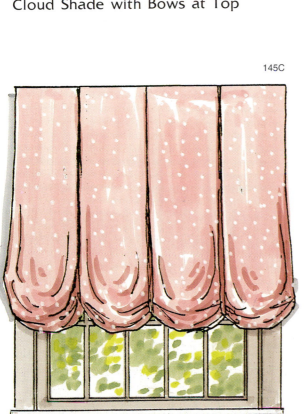

Balloon Shade

Balloon Shade with Shirred
Cornice Box

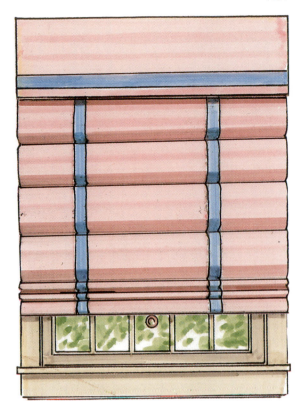

Roman Shade with Valance

Roman Shade with Banding

Continental Cloud with Ruffles

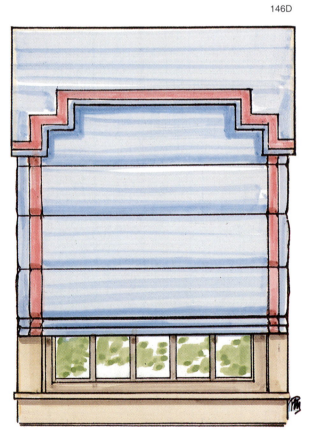

Valance over Roman Shade

DECORATING TERMS & INFORMATION

A

"A" Frame Window — Very contemporary house structures sometimes forms an "A" shape. When draperies are used, they hang from the cross-beam of the "A," or they can be fabricated and installed to conform to the shape of the window.

Allowance — A customary variation from an "exact" measurement, taken for the purpose of anticipated needs.

Apron — A piece of wood trim beneath the window sill.

B

Bar-Tack — A sewing machine operation of repeated stitches concentrated to secure the lowest portion of drapery pleats.

Baton — A rod or wand used to hand draw traverse draperies.

Bay Window — A large projecting type of window made of a group of windows set at angles to each other and joined to each other on some sides.

Bottom Hem — The turned part forming a finished edge at bottom of drapery.

Bow Window — A large projecting type of window that is curved or semi-circular.

Box Pleat — A fold of cloth sewn into place to create fullness in a drapery. Box pleats are evenly spaced and stitched.

Bracket — Metal piece attached to the wall or casing to support a drapery or curtain rod.

C

Cafe — A traversing or non-traversing drapery, designed as a tier. The heading can be various styles. They can be set at a variety of heights to control ventilation, view and light.

Cafe Rod — A small, round decorative rod which comes in white, brass or woodgrain finish, used to mount cafe curtains that do not have a rod pocket. Cafe rods are meant to be seen and add an additional decorative touch to the curtain treatment.

Canopy — A fabric window topper created by sewing pockets into fabric panels and inserting a rod with a small projection at the top of the panel, a rod with a larger projection at the bottom.

Cantonniere — A three-sided shaped or straight cornice that "frames" the window — across the top and down the two sides. It is made of a hardboard, padded and covered with fabric.

Carriers — Small runners installed in a traverse rod which hold a drapery pin or hook.

Cartridge Pleat — A fold of cloth sewn into place to create fullness in a drapery. This is a round pleat 2-2½ inches in depth. Roundness is created by stuffing of crinoline or paper (removed for cleaning).

Cascade — A fall of fabric that descends in a zig-zag line from a drapery heading or top treatment.

Casement — (1) A cloth drapery that is of an open-weave material but more opaque than a sheer. (2) A type of vertically hinged window, whose panes open by sliding sideways or cranking outward.

Casing (Window) — Wooden frame around a window.

Center Draw — One pair of draperies which draws open and closes exactly at a window's center point.

Center Support — A metal grip which is used to support a traverse rod from above and prevents rod from sagging in the middle, but does not interfere with rod operation.

Clerestory Windows — A series of small windows which let in light and air. These are placed high on the wall to allow complete privacy.

Corner Window

Corner Window — A corner window literally wraps a corner of the building at right angles.

Cornice — A shallow, box-like structure, usually made of wood, fastened across the top of a window to conceal the drapery hardware.

Crinoline — A heavily sized, stiff fabric used as a foundation to support the edge of a hem or puffed sleeve. Also used as interlining.

Custom-Made Draperies — Draperies made to order in a workroom or decorator shop.

Cut Length — The cut length of the fabric is the length after allowances have been made for heading and hem.

D

Dormer Window — A dormer window is an upright window which breaks the surface of a sloping roof.

Double Hung — May be several items: Double hung window, Double hung shutters, and Double hung draperies (two sets of draperies usually sheer fabric under opaque fabric, both operating independently).

Draw Draperies — Panels of fabric, featuring pleated headings.

E

End Bracket — The two supporting metal grips which hold a drapery rod to the wall or ceiling. They control the amount of projection.

End Housing — Refers to the box parts at the extreme ends of a traverse drapery rod. They enclose the mechanism through which the cords run.

F

Fenestration — Location and proportion of windows in relationship to solid wall areas.

Festoon — A decorative drapery treatment of folded fabric that hangs in a graceful curve, and frames the top of a window.

Finial — Decorative end piece on cafe rods or decorative traverse rods (also referred to as "pole ends").

Finished Length — This is the length after draperies have been made, using the extra allowances in hem and heading.

French Pleats — This is a three-fold pleat and the one most often used in draperies.

H

Heading — The hemmed, usually stiffened, portion across the top of a curtain or drapery.

Hem — Refers to finished sides and bottom edges of a drapery.

Holdback — A decorative piece of hardware that holds draperies to each side of the window.

I

Insert Pulley — An auxiliary traverse rod part, over which the cords operate.

J

Jabot — A decorative vertical end of an over treatment that usually finishes a horizontal festoon.

Jamb — Interior sides of a door or window frame.

L

Lambrequin — A cornice that completely frames the window. Sometimes used interchangeably with valance or cantonniere.

Laminated Weights — Weight covered on both sides to avoid rust marks on drapery.

Lanai — A type of window covering made up of a series of hinged, rigid plastic panels, hung from a traverse track.

Lining — A fabric backing for a drapery.

Lintel — Lintels are wood, steel, or reinforced concrete beams placed over both window and door openings to hold up the wall and roof above.

M

Master Carrier — Two arms that overlap in center of rod when draperies are closed, allowing draperies to close completely.

Milium — Trade name for a thermal lining.

Mitered Corner — The formation of the bottom edge of drapery with a 45 degree angle on hem side.

Mullion — The vertical wood or masonry sections between a series of window frames.

Multi-Draw — A simultaneous opening and closing of several draperies on one rod at one time.

Muntin — The horizontal wood strips that separate panes of glass in windows.

O

Off-Center — A window not centered on a wall. Draperies still meet at its center point.

One-Way Draw — Drapery designed to draw one way only, in one panel.

Open Cuff — This is on the back side of drapery and at top. Open cuffs make one of the strongest type headings on any drapery. This results when you carry both fabrics to the top and make a turn with the crinoline.

Overlap — The overlap of a pair of draperies is that part of a drapery panel which rides the master carrier of a traverse rod and overlaps in the center when draperies are drawn closed. Usually 3½'' on each side.

P

Panel — One half a pair of draperies or curtains.

Pattern Repeat — The ''repeat'' of a pattern is the distance between any given point in a design to where that exact point is repeated again.

Picture Window — A type of window with a large center glass area with usually two smaller glass areas on each side.

Pin-On-Hook — A metal pin to fasten draperies to a rod. It pins into drapery pleat and hooks to traverse carrier or cafe rod.

Pinch Pleats — A drapery heading where the basic pleat is divided into two or three smaller, equal pleats, sewn together at the bottom edge on the right side of the fabric.

Pleat — A fold of cloth sewn into place to create fullness.

Pleat To — ''Pleat To'' is the finished width of the fabric after it has been pleated. Example: A width of 48'' fabric has been pleated to 18'' — ''Pleat To'' 18''.

Pleater Tape — Pocketed heading material designed to be used with pleating hooks.

Projection — Refers to a jutting out, an extension. On a curtain or drapery rod, it is that part which returns to the wall from the front of the rod.

Protractor — A drapery tool by which exact angles are measured (as in bay windows).

R

Ready-Mades — Standard size draperies, factory-made and available at local stores or through mail order sources.

Repeat — The space from one design motif to the next one on a patterned fabric.

Return — The distance from the face of the rod to the wall or casing where the bracket is attached.

Rod Pocket — A hollow sleeve in the top — and sometimes the bottom — of a curtain or drapery through which a rod is inserted. The rod is then attached to a solid wall surface.

S

Sash Curtain — Any sheer material hung close to the window glass. Usually hung from spring tension rods or sash rods mounted inside the window casing.

Sash Rod — A small rod, either decorative or plain, usually mounted inside a window frame on the sash.

Scalloped Heading — A popular top treatment for cafe curtains featuring semi-circular spaces between curtain rings.

Selvedge — The tightly woven edge on a width of fabric to hold the fabric together.

Side Hem — The turned part forming a finished edge at the side of the drapery.

Sill — The horizontal ''ledge-like'' portion of a window casing.

Slides — Small runners installed in a traverse rod which hold a drapery pin or hook.

Spacing — Refers to the flat space between pleats; the fuller the drapery, the less the spacing.

Stacking — The area required for draperies when they are completely opened.

Swag — A section of draped fabric above a window.

T

Tension Pulley — The pulley attachment through which the traverse cords move for one continuous smooth operation when drapery is drawn. May be mounted on baseboard, casing or wall, on one or both sides.

Tiebacks — Decorative pieces of hardware, sometimes called holdbacks. Available in many forms and designed to hold draperies back from the window to allow light passage or add an additional decorative touch to the window treatment.

Tier — Curtain layers arranged one above the other with a normal overlap of 4''. Upper tiers project from the wall at a greater distance than lower panel to allow each curtain to hang free.

Traverse — To draw across. A traverse drapery is one that opens or closes across a window by means of the traverse rod from which it is hung.

U

Under-Draperies — A lightweight drapery, usually a sheer, closest to the window glass. It hangs beneath a heavier over-drapery.

V

Valance — A valance is a horizontal decorative fabric treatment used at the top of draperies to screen hardware and cords.

W

Weights — (chain and lead) Lead weights are sewn in at the vertical seams and each corner of drapery panel. Chain weights are small beads strung in a line along bottom hemline of sheers, to insure an even hemline and straight hanging.

Width — A word to describe a single width of fabric. Several widths of fabric are sewn together to make a panel of drapery. ''Panel'' is sometimes used in referring to a width of fabric.

Glossary of Fabrics and Fabric Terms

A

Antique Satin — One of the most common drapery fabrics sold. Characterized by a lustrous effect, normally composed of rayon/acetate blends.

B

Basketweave — Plain under-and-over weave; primarily in draperies.

Batiste — A soft finished fabric which has a high count of fine yarns. It is more opaque than voiles. Usually composed of 100% polyester or a polyester blend.

"Beta" Fiberglas Fiber — This filament is around .00010 inch in diameter, about one half the diameter of other glass fibers in use at present. Properties include improved flexibility, greater resistance to mechanical abuse to afford greater wearability, increased softness and suppleness and less irritation. "Beta" is used in apparel, home furnishings, and industrial fields. A registered trademark name of Owens-Corning Fiberglas Corp., N.Y.C.

Boucle — French for curled, indicates a curled or looped surface.

Brocade — Rich jacquard — woven fabric with all-over interwoven design of raised figures or flowers. Brocade has a raised surface in contrast to felt damask, and is generally made of silk, rayon and nylon yarns with or without metallic treatment.

Burlap — Coarse, canvas-like fabric made of jute, hemp or cotton. Also called Gunny.

C

Casements — Open weave casual fabric, characterized by its instability.

Challis — One of the softest fabrics made. Normally made of rayon and also combined with cotton.

Chintz — Glazed cotton fabric often printed with gay figures and large flower designs. Some glazes will wash out in laundering. The only durable glaze is a resin finish which will withstand washing or dry cleaning. Unglazed chintz is called cretonne.

Corduroy — A cut filling-pile cloth with narrow to wide wales which run in the warp direction of the goods and made possible by the use of an extra set of filling yarns in the construction. The back is of plain or twill weave, the latter affording the better construction. Washable types are available and stretch and durable press garments of corduroy are very popular. Usually an all-cotton cloth, some of the goods are now made with nylon or rayon pile effect on a cotton backing fabric or with polyester-cotton blends.

Crash — A coarse fabric having a rough irregular surface obtained by weavig thick uneven yarns. Usually cotton or linen, sometimes spun rayon or blends.

Crinoline — A heavily sized, stiff fabric used as a foundation to support the edge of a hem or puffed sleeve. Also used as interlining.

D

Damask — Firm, glossy jacquard-patterned fabric. Damask is similar to brocade, but flatter and reversible. It can be made from linen, cotton, rayon or silk, or a combination of fibers.

Double Knit — A fabric knitted with a double stitch on a double needle frame to provide a double thickness and is the same on both sides. It has excellent body and stability.

F

Faille — Plain weave (flat-rib); with filling yarns heavier than warp.

Foamback — Term used to denote that a fabric has been laminated to a backing of polyurethane foam.

G

Glasing — Thin finish provides luster, sheen, shine or polish to some fabrics. Chintz is an example of a glazed fabric.

H

Hand, Handle — The reaction of the sense of touch, when fabrics are held in the hand. There are many factors which give "character or individuality" to a material observed through handling. A correct judgement may thus be made concerning its capabilities in content, working properties, drapability, feel, elasticity, fineness and softness, launderability, etc.

I

Inherent Flame Frees — Fabric woven of flame-resistant fabric (not processed) and flame-free for life of the fabric.

L

Linen — This is a product of the flax plant. Among the properties of linen are rapid moisture absorption, no fuzziness, does not soil quickly, a natural luster and stiffness.

M

Matelasse — Appearance of a quilted weave; figured pattern with a raised, bubbly surface.

Modacrylic — A modified fiber in which the fiber-forming substance of any longchain synthetic polymer is composed of less than 85%, but at least 25% of weight of acrylonitrile units.

Mohair — Comes from the Angora goat, one of the oldest animals known to man. It is lighter weight drapery fabric; slightly brushed or hairy finish.

Moire — A finish given cotton, silk, acetate, rayon, nylon, etc., where bright and dim effects are observed. This is achieved by passing the fabric between engraved rollers which press the particular motif into the fabric.

N

Ninon — A smooth, transparent, high textured type of voile fabric. Usually made from 100% polyester.

O

Ombre — A graduate or shade effect of color used in a striped motif. Usually ranges from light to dark tones.

Organdy — Very light and thin, transparent, stiff and wiry cotton cloth. Will withstand repeated launderings and still retain its crispness. Organdy is a true, durable finish cloth.

Satin Weave — One of the three basic weaves, the others being plain weave and the twill weave. The surface of satin weave cloth is almost made up entirely of warp or filling floats since in the repeat of the weave, each yarn of the one system passes or floats over or under all but one yarn of the opposite yarn system. Satin weaves have a host of uses — brocade, brocatelle, damask other decorative materials.

Selvage — Each side edge of a woven fabric and an actual part of the warp in the goods. Other names for it are listing, self-edge, and raw edge.

Silk — The only natural fiber that comes in a filament form, reeled from the cocoon, cultivated or wild.

Slub Yarn — Yarn of any type which is irregular in diameter; may be caused by error, or purposely made with slubs to bring out some desired effect to enhance a material.

T

Taffeta — A fine plain weave fabric smooth on both sides, usually with a sheen on its surface.

Terry Cloth — This cloth fabric has uncut loops on both sides of the cloth. Terry is also made on a Jacquard loom to form interesting motifs.

Texture — The first meaning is the actual number of warp threads and filling picks per inch in any cloth that has been woven. Texture is also much used by the public and in advertising circles to mean the finish and appearance of cloth.

Thread Count — 1. The actual number of warp ends and filling picks per inch in a woven cloth. Texture is another name for this term. 2. In knitted fabric, thread count implies the number of wales or ribs, and the courses per inch.

V

Velour — 1. A term loosely applied to cut pile cloths in general; also to fabrics with a fine raised finish. 2. A cut pile cotton fabric comparable with cotton velvet, but with a greater and denser pile. 3. A staple, high grade woolen fabric which has a close, fine, dense, erect, and even nap which provides a soft, pleasing hand.

Velvet — A warp pile cloth in which a succession of rows of short cut pile stand so close together as to give an even, uniform surface. When the pile is more than one-eighth of an inch high, the cloth is usually called plus.

Voile — A thin open mesh cloth made by a variation of plain weave. Most voiles are made of polyester. Similar to ninon, but with a much finer denier of yarn with a very soft, drapable hand.

W

Warp — The yarns which run vertically or lengthwise in woven fabric.

Weft Yarn — The yarn runs horizontal or cross yarns.

Drapery Fabrics — Look & Performance

Satins and Jacquards
Usually the most formal and traditional, they are generally made from tightly woven, heavy, soft material which hangs straight from top to bottom in (formal) folds.

Casements, Open Weaves
These have a lighter, more casual feel. They are usually made from loosely woven, textured yarns that hang in looser folds than the formal satins and Jacquards.

Sheers
Made of soft, see-through fabrics, sheers are appropriate in most decors. Light and airy, they are sometimes used in combination with heavier draperies in more formal settings. They are billowy unless weighted, and can be made to drape quite well.

Prints
Suitable in most decors, prints are made from a light, tightly woven fabric, usually cotton or cotton-polyester blends.

Drapery Linings
Linings add substantially to the luxurious appearance necessary for good window treatments, and also provide a fuller pleated look for maintaining a soft drapable hand.

The lined-look provides uniformity to the exterior appearance of a home while allowing a broad choice of textures, weaves, colors and patterns for the interior.

The combination of sunlight and air pollution will eventually take its toll on all colors. There is no such thing as an absolutely colorfast material or dye. Some colors, however will show fading more dramatically than others. Bright colors tend to show fading more than subdued tones, and solids before prints.

Linings help draperies last longer. They afford some protection against sun and fading. They also protect the draperies from water stains — either from condensation on the inside of the window or from a sudden shower.

Insulated linings contribute to energy conservation, keeping homes cooler in summer and warmer in winter.

Textile Fibers & Their Properties

NATURAL FIBERS

COTTON

Drapability:	excellent hang, soft hand
Color fastness:	good, vat dyes best
Sun resistance:	excellent, does not sun rot
Abrasion resistance:	excellent
Sagging:	does not stretch, except when wet
Resiliency:	poor, packs easily, wrinkles easily, very absorbent, burns
Care:	wash or dry clean and iron at high temperature

Cotton generally wears excellently in drapery (print or plains).

LINEN OR FLAX

Drapability:	good hang, but not as soft as cotton
Color fastness:	good to poor, prints do not hold their color as well as plain fabrics
Sun resistance:	excellent, does not sun rot
Abrasion resistance:	excellent
Sagging:	strong, does not stretch
Resiliency:	poor, packs badly, does wrinkle
Care:	dry clean and iron at high temperature

Linens are excellent in plain and casement fabric and good in prints.

SILK

Drapability:	good hang, medium to soft hand
Color fastness:	good
Sun resistance:	poor, rots in short time, lining helps
Abrasion resistance:	good
Sagging:	strong, does not sag
Resiliency:	good, does not pack badly
Care:	dry clean and iron at medium temperature

Little silk is used in drapery today. This is due to sun rot and cost.

WOOL

There is virtually none used in drapery fabric.

MAN-MADE

RAYON

Drapability:	good hang, soft hand
Color fastness:	good to excellent (solution dyed)
Sun resistance:	good, but not as good as cotton or linen
Abrasion resistance:	good, but not as good as nylon or cotton
Sagging:	poor, stretches in loose yarns, but OK in tight woven fabrics
Resiliency:	good, does not pack, wrinkles less than cotton or linen
Care:	dry clean and iron at medium temperature

Rayon is blended with other fibers: cotton, acetate and linen.

ACETATE

Drapability:	good hand, soft hand
Color fastness:	good (solution dyed)
Sun resistance:	good, not as good as cotton and linen
Abrasion resistance:	good, but not as good as cotton or nylon
Sagging:	poor stretches in loose yarns, but OK in tight woven fabrics
Resiliency:	good, does not pack, wrinkles less than cotton or linen
Care:	dry clean and iron at low temperature

Blends well with other fibers, rayon and nylon.

POLYESTER

Drapability:	excellent hang, very soft hand
Color fastness:	good to excellent
Sun resistance:	excellent
Abrasion resistance:	good, sheers must be handled with care. Fabric can be bruised.
Sagging:	excellent, does not stretch or shrink
Resiliency:	good to excellent, does not pack, wrinkle free
Care:	wash or dry clean and iron at low temperature temperature

Polyester is an excellent fabric for most drapery applications. It blends well with other fibers. In polyester cotton blends, cotton wrinkles less.

NYLON

Drapability:	good, soft to stiff hand, not as soft as polyesters
Color fastness:	good to excellent
Sun resistance:	poor
Abrasion resistance:	excellent
Sagging:	excellent, does not sag
Resiliency:	excellent, does not pack, wrinkle free
Care:	dry clean and iron at low temperature

Nylon is not widely used in drapery fabric.

ACRYLIC

Drapability:	excellent, very soft hand
Color fastness:	excellent, if solution dyed
Sun resistance:	excellent, good as cotton or linen
Abrasion resistance:	good
Sagging:	very good, does not stretch
Resiliency:	very good, does not pack and wrinkle free
Care:	dry clean and iron at low temperature 50°

Acrylic fabrics hang well and do not sag. Can be blended with polyester. Modacrylics are flameproof.

DYNEL

Drapability:	excellent, soft hand like acrylic
Color fastness:	excellent
Sun resistance:	good to excellent
Abrasion resistance:	excellent
Sagging:	excellent compared to rayon or acetate
Resiliency:	very good, does not pack, wrinkle free, low flamability
Care:	Wash only, ironing does not affect it much, use low heat

Basic Window Types

1. **Double Hung Window** — Most common of all window types, has two sashes, one or both of which slide up and down. Unless it is too long and narrow or in the wrong location, this type of window is usually one of the easiest to decorate.

2. **In-Swinging Casement** — Opens into the room. If it is not decorated properly, curtains and draperies may tangle with the window as it is opened and closed.

3. **Out-Swinging Casement** — Opens outward. Both in-swinging and out-swinging casements may be operated by a crank, or simply moved by hand. Out-swinging casements are easily decorated.

4. **Ranch or Strip Windows** — Most often a wide window set high off the floor. Usually has sliding sashes and is common to most ranch type houses. It requires special consideration when decorating to make it attractive.

5. **Awning Window** — Has wide, horizontal sashes that open outward to any angle; can usually be left open when it's raining. Unless it is awkwardly placed or shaped, it's an easy one to decorate.

6. **Jalousie Window** — Identified by narrow, horizontal strips of glass that open by means of a crank to any desired angle. Decorating problems result only when the shape or location is unusual.

7. **Picture Window** — One designed to frame an outside view. It may consist of one large, fixed pane of glass, in which case the window cannot be opened. Or it may have movable sections on one or both sides of a fixed pane — or above and below — which can be opened for ventilation. Sometimes there are decorating problems, but in general, a picture window is your big opportunity.

8. **Dormer Window** — Usually a small window projecting from the house in an alcove-like extension of the room. It requires a treatment all its own.

9. **Bay Windows** — Three or more windows set at an angle to each other in a recessed area. You can use lots of imagination with bay windows.

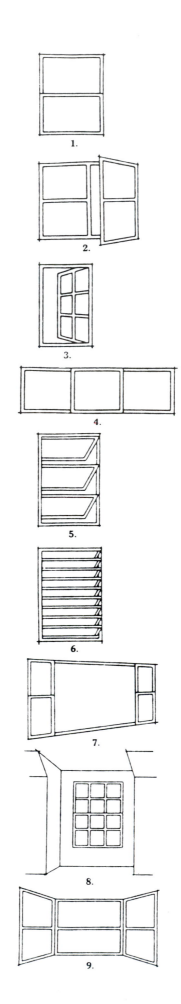

10. **Bow Window** — A curved window, sometimes called a circular bay.

11. **Slanting Window** — Often called "cathedral" window, usually an entire wall of the room. Its main characteristic is the angle at the top where the window follows the line of a slanting roof. This top slanting line often causes decorating concern, but the problem can be solved very effectively.

12. **Double Windows** — Side by side windows. (If there are more than one they are often called multiple windows.) Most often treated as a single unit, always think of them together, as one decorating element.

13. **Corner Windows** — Any window that comes together at the corner of a room.

14. **French Doors** — Sometimes called French windows. They come in pairs and often open onto a porch or patio. Usually they need special decorating to look their best.

15. **Sliding Glass Doors** — Today's functional version of French doors. They are often set into a regular wall, but are sometimes part of a modern "glass wall." Either way, they need special decor that allows them to serve as doors yet provide nighttime privacy.

16. **Clerestory Window** — A shallow window set near the ceiling. Usually should be decorated inconspicuously. (In modern architecture, it is sometimes placed in the slope of a beamed ceiling, in which case it should rarely be decorated at all.)

17. **Palladian Window** — An arched top window with straight panes below the arch.

18 **Glass Wall** — Usually a group of basic window units made to fit together, forming a veritable "wall" of windows. Curtains and draperies often require special planning.

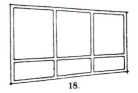

Custom Made Draperies

Standard Workmanship and Quality Features

- Double Heading
- 4" Permanent Buckram Headings
- Pleating custom tacked with extra thread
- All seams serged and overlocked
- All draperies perfectly matched
- All draperies table sized
- Blind stitched bottom and side hems
- Double 4" bottom hems + 1½" Double side hems
- All draperies weighted at corners and seams.
- Multiple width draperies are pleated so that joining seams are hidden behind pleats.

Made to Custom Measurements

To any exact width or length.
Pleated to any desired fullness up to 3 to 1.
Lined or unlined.

Drapery Terminology

- Width is one strip of material (can be any length) which can be pleated to a finished dimension across the TOP of between 16" and 24". Using a 48" wide material as our base, a width of which finishes to 24" is considered double fullness or 2 to 1; 16" finished width is considered triple fullness or 3 to 1. Any number of widths can be joined together to make the draperies properly cover the window area.
- Panel is a single unit of drapery of one or more widths, which is used specifically for one way draw — stack left or stack right — and/or stationary units.
- Pair is two equal panels which are pleated to cover a desired area.
- Return is the measurement from the rod to the wall; in other words the projection.
- Overlap is the measurement, when draperies are fully closed, of having the right panel overlap the left panel. This is usually 3" for each panel. *Remember your customer must add 12" to the rod measurement to insure proper returns and overlaps.*

Options Available on Draperies

A variety of Headings:
Pinch Pleated with 4" buckram
Pinch Pleated with 5" buckram
Box Pleated
Box Pleated with Tabs for rod. Add diameter of rod to finished length. For flat tab draperies use 2-1.
Rod Pocket for shirred draperies.
Draperies may be self-lined, or
Draperies may be lined with black-out lining.

Pleat Spacing

Pleat spacings vary according to the widths of material used to achieve a specified finished width. For example: 3 widths of material pleated to 59 inches to the pair will not have the same pleat spacing as 3 widths of material pleated to 72 inches to the pair. If pleats and pleat spacing are to look alike on draperies of different widths, please specify "comparable fullness" on your order. *Vertically striped fabrics will not fabricate to allow an identical stripe to fall between each pleat, panel to panel, or pair to pair.*

How to Order Your Draperies

Since "Made-to-Measure" draperies are made to your exact specifications it is imperative that measurements be made with the greatest of care. We recommend that you double check all measurements for accuracy. All measuring should be done with a steel tape or yardstick. Measure each window separately even when they appear to be the same size. If length varies use dimension of shortest length.

Drapery Width

- Measure width of drapery rod from end to end.
- Add to this figure an extra 12" to include the allowance for standard traverse rod returns and overlap.
- Standard returns are 3" in depth. For over-draperies allow for clearance of under-curtain. A 6" return should be sufficient.
- When ordering panels that stack (draw) in one direction only, specify if the drapery is to stack (draw) left or right.

Drapery Length

- Measure from top of rod, to floor or to carpet. (By inserting pins 1" from top drapery will automatically clear the floor or carpet.)
- Under-curtain should be at least ½" shorter than over-drapery.
- When floor length draperies are used it is best to measure length at each side and in the center. Use shortest figure for your measurement.
- Rod should be placed a minimum of 4" above the window so hooks and pleats will not be observed from outside.
- If sill length, allow 4" below sill so bottom hem will not be observed from outside.
- When using pole rings, measure length from bottom of rings.

Caution: When both under-curtain and over-drapery are used, be sure to allow for clearance of face drapery. For example, an under-curtain with a 3½" return requires at least a 6" return on the over-drapery.

PLEAT-TO / FULLNESS CHARTS

(48'' Fabric) 2½ X's Fullness

PLEAT-TO	19	38	57	76	95	114	133	152	171	190	209	228	247	266	285
WIDTHS	1	2	3	4	5	6	7	8	9	10	11	12	13	14	15

(48'' Fabric) 3 X's Fullness

PLEAT-TO	15	30	45	60	75	90	105	120	135	150	165	180	195	210	225
WIDTHS	1	2	3	4	5	6	7	8	9	10	11	12	13	14	15

(54'' Fabric) 2½ X's Fullness

PLEAT-TO	21	42	63	84	105	126	147	168	189	210	231	254	273	294	315
WIDTHS	1	2	3	4	5	6	7	8	9	10	11	12	13	14	15

(54'' Fabric) 3 X's Fullness

PLEAT-TO	17	34	51	68	85	102	119	136	153	170	187	204	221	238	255
WIDTHS	1	2	3	4	5	6	7	8	9	10	11	12	13	14	15

FULLNESS CHART

48'' Fabric	Pleated to 2½ X's fullness = 19'' Panels
54'' Fabric	Pleated to 2½ X's fullness = 21'' Panels
60'' Fabric	Pleated to 2½ X's fullness = 23'' Panels

48'' Fabric	Pleated to 3 X's fullness = 15'' Panels
54'' Fabric	Pleated to 3 X's fullness = 17'' Panels
60'' Fabric	Pleated to 3 X's fullness = 19'' Panels

48'' Fabric	Pleated to 2 X's fullness = 23'' Panels
54'' Fabric	Pleated to 2 X's fullness = 26'' Panels
60'' Fabric	Pleated to 2 X's fullness = 29'' Panels

PLEAT TO CHART

Heavy Duty Rods

Oneway 3½'' return add 5 inches
Center Open 3½ return add 12 inches

One Way 6'' return add 7 inches
Center Open 6'' return add 16 inches

Decorator Type Rods

One Way 3½'' return add 7 inches
Center Open 3½'' add 16 inches

One Way 6'' return add 9 inches
Center Open 6'' return add 19 inches

STACK BACK CHART

IF THE GLASS IS	TOTAL STACK-BACK SHOULD BE	ROD LENGTH AND DRAPERY COVERAGE SHOULD BE
38 inches	26 inches	64 inches
44	28	72
50	30	80
56	32	88
62	34	96
68	36	104
75	37	112
81	39	120
87	41	128
94	42	136
100	44	144
106	46	152
112	48	160
119	49	168
125	51	176
131	53	184
137	55	192
144	56	200
150	58	208
156	60	216
162	62	224
169	63	232
175	65	240
181	67	248
187	69	255

NOTE: You will have to ADD RETURNS AND OVERLAPS TO DRAPERY COVERAGE.

THIS CHART IS BASED ON AVERAGE PLEATING AND MEDIUM WEIGHT FABRIC. YOU MAY DEDUCT 7" FROM ROD LENGTH IF YOU ARE USING A ONE WAY ROD. IF BULKY FABRIC IS USED, ADD TO STACK-BACK ACCORDINGLY.

YARDAGE CHART FOR 4" OR 5" HEADING (Cut Plus 20")
TOTAL NUMBER OF WIDTHS PER PAIR OR PANEL

FINISHED LENGTH	36"	40"	44"	48"	52"	56"	60"	64"	68"	72"	76"	80"	84"	88"	92"	96"	100"	104"	108"
15W	22¾	23	26½	26¾	30	31¼	33½	35	36¾	38½	40	41¾	43½	45	46¾	48½	50	51¾	53½
14W	21¼	21½	24¼	25	28	29¾	31¼	32¾	34¼	36	37½	39	40½	42	43¾	45¼	46¾	48¼	50
13W	19¾	20	23	23¼	26	27½	29	30½	32	33¼	34¾	36¼	37¾	39	40½	42	43½	45	46¼
12W	18¼	18½	21¼	21½	24	25½	26¾	28	29½	30¾	32	33½	34¾	36	37½	38¾	40	41½	42¾
11W	16¾	17	19½	19¾	22	23¼	24½	25¾	27	28¼	29½	30¾	32	33	34¼	35½	36¾	38	39¼
10W	15¼	15½	17¾	18	20	21¼	22¼	23½	24½	25¾	26¾	28	29	30	31¼	32¼	33½	34½	35¾
9W	13¾	14	16	16¼	18	19	20	21	22	23	24	25	26	27	28	29	30	31	32
8W	12¼	12½	14¼	14½	16	16¾	18	18¾	19¾	20½	21½	22¼	23¼	24	25	26	26¾	27¾	28½
7W	10¾	11	12½	12¾	14	15	15¾	16½	17¼	18	18¾	19½	20¼	21	22	22¾	23½	24¼	25
6W	9¼	9½	10¾	11	12	12¾	13½	14	14¾	15½	16	16¾	17½	18	18¾	19½	20	20¾	21½
5W	7¾	8	9	9¼	10	10¾	11¼	11¾	12¼	13	13½	14	14½	15	15¾	16¼	16¾	17¼	18
4W	6¼	6½	7¼	7½	8	8½	9	9½	10	10¼	10¾	11¼	11¾	12	12½	13	13½	14	14¼
3W	4¾	5	5½	5¾	6	6½	6¾	7	7½	7¾	8	8½	8¾	9	9½	9¾	10	10½	10¾
2W	3¼	3½	3¾	4	4	4¼	4½	4¾	5	5¼	5½	5¾	6	6	6¼	6½	6¾	7	7¼

RTB . . . . Cut Plus 12"   TIE BACKS . . . . CUT 12"
YARDAGE CHART FOR 5" HEADINGS (DOUBLE) . . . PLAIN FABRICS ONLY. CUT PLUS 20".

157

Fabric Shade Measuring Information

Inside Installation

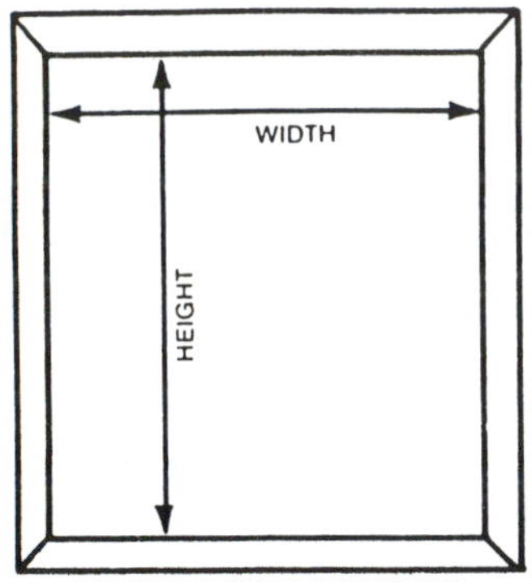

INSIDE OR RECESSED MOUNT

A. Width: Measure width of window at the top, center and bottom of window, and use narrowest measurement when ordering. Specify on order form if inside clearance has been made. If no clearance has been allowed factory will deduct ¼" from overall width.

B. Length: Measure height of window from top of opening to top of sill, no allowance is made for length.

Outside Installation

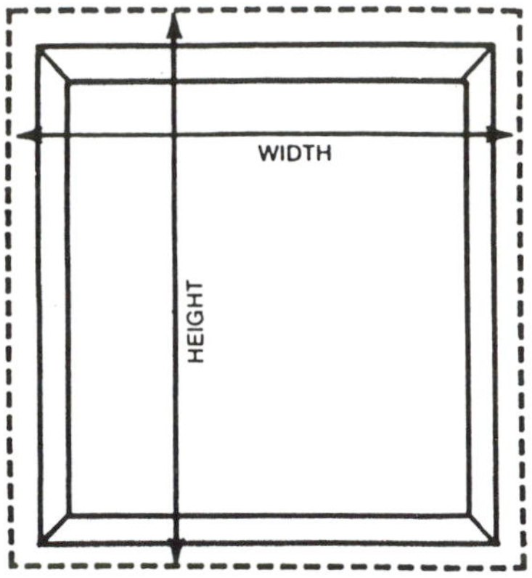

OUTSIDE OR WALL MOUNT

A. Width: Measure exact width of area to be covered. It is recommended that shades extend past actual window opening by 2" on each side. Furnish finished shade width, no allowances will be made.

B. Length: Measure length of area to be covered, allowing a minimum of 2½" at top of window to accomodate headerboard and brackets. (At this time you may want to take into consideration stackage of shades and allow for this in your length measurement.) Furnish finished shade length, no allowance will be made.

ALL INSTALLATIONS

A. Specify right or left cord position. If no cord position is indicated, cords will be corded to right hand side.

B. Specify cord length (length of cord needed for easy reach, when shade is completely down). If no specification is made, cord length will be approximately ⅓ length of shade.

C. For Pole Cloud, Cloud and Balloon shades, specify if length given is high or low point of pouff.

Square Footage Chart

SHADE LENGTH *in inches*	SHADE WIDTH *in inches*																				
	24	30	36	42	48	54	60	66	72	78	84	90	96	102	108	114	120	126	132	138	144
30	10	10	10	10	10	11¼	12½	13¾	15	16¼	17½	18¾	20	21¼	22½	23¾	25	26¼	27½	28¾	30
36	10	10	10	10½	12	13½	15	16½	18	19½	21	22½	24	25½	27	28½	30	31½	33	34½	36
42	10	10	10½	12¼	14	15¾	17½	19¼	21	22¾	24½	26¼	28	29¾	31½	33¼	35	36¾	38½	40¼	42
48	10	10	12	14	16	18	20	22	24	26	28	30	32	34	36	38	40	42	44	46	48
54	10	11¼	13½	15¾	18	20¼	22½	24¾	27	29¼	31½	33¾	36	38¼	40½	42¾	45	47¼	49½	51¾	54
60	10	12½	15	17½	20	22½	25	27½	30	32½	35	37½	40	42½	45	47½	50	52½	55	57½	60
66	11	13¾	16½	19¼	22	24¾	27½	30¼	33	35¾	38½	41¼	44	46¾	49½	52¼	55	57¾	60½	63¼	66
72	12	15	18	21	24	27	30	33	36	39	42	45	48	51	54	57	60	63	66	69	72
78	13	16¼	19½	22¾	26	29¼	32½	35¾	39	42¼	45½	48¾	52	55¼	58½	61¾	65	68¼	71½	74¾	78
84	14	17½	21	24½	28	31½	35	38½	42	45½	49	52½	56	59½	63	66½	70	73½	77	80½	84
90	15	18¾	22½	26¼	30	33¾	37½	41¼	45	48¾	52½	56¼	60	63¾	67½	71¼	75	78¾	82½	86¼	90
96	16	20	24	28	32	36	40	44	48	52	56	60	64	68	72	76	80	84	88	92	96
102	17	21¼	25½	29¾	34	38¼	42½	46¾	51	55¼	59½	63¾	68	72¼	76½	80¾	85	89¼	93½	97¾	102
108	18	22½	27	31½	36	40½	45	49½	54	58½	63	67½	72	76½	81	85½	90	94½	99	103½	108
114	19	23¾	28½	33¼	38	42¾	47½	52¼	57	61¾	66½	71¼	76	80¾	85½	90¼	95	99¾	104½	109¼	114
120	20	25	30	35	40	45	50	55	60	65	70	75	80	85	90	95	100	105	110	115	120
126	21	26¼	31½	36¾	42	47¼	52½	57¾	63	68¼	73½	78¾	84	89¼	94½	99¾	105	110¼	115½	120¾	126
132	22	27½	33	38½	44	49½	55	60½	66	71½	77	82½	88	93½	99	104½	110	115½	121	126½	132
138	23	28¾	34½	40¼	46	51¾	57½	63¼	69	74¾	80½	86¼	92	97¾	103½	109¼	115	120¾	126½	132¼	138
144	24	30	36	42	48	54	60	66	72	78	84	90	96	102	108	114	120	126	132	138	144